CULTURES OF THE WORLD

Indonesia

Marshall Cavendish
Benchmark
New York

PICTURE CREDITS

Cover: ©dbimages/Alamy
Andrew Brownbill/Lonely Planet Images: 5 • Bernard Napthine/Lonely Planet Images: 36, 121 • Christopher Groenhout/Lonely Planet Images: 131 • Edy Purnomo/Getty Images: 47 • Felix Hug/Lonely Planet Images: 18, 107, 108 • Frank Carter/Lonely Planet Images: 116 • Greg Elms/Lonely Planet Images: 120 • Inmagine: 17, 22, 23, 26, 29, 30, 42, 44, 45, 62, 66, 69, 88, 89, 91, 98, 103, 106, 109, 117, 118, 124, 126, 128 • Jane Sweeney/Lonely Planet Images: 10, 43 • Jerry Alexander/Lonely Planet Images: 46, 70, 90, 125 • Jewel Samad/AFP/Getty Images: 8 • Karl Lehmann/Lonely Planet Images: 19 • Liu Jin/AFP/Getty Images: 110 • Marshall Cavendish International (Asia): 135 • Michael Coyne/Lonely Planet Images: 78 • Oscar Siagian/Getty Images: 37 • Paul Beinssen/Lonely Planet Images: 38, 48 • Paul Kennedy/Lonely Planet Images: 80 • Peter Ptschelinzew/Lonely Planet Images: 34, 51, 68, 94 • photolibrary: 1, 3, 6, 7, 9, 11, 13, 15, 20, 24, 50, 52, 53, 54, 57, 58, 73, 82, 84, 86, 97, 100, 101, 102, 112, 113, 114, 115, 122, 123, 130 • Rachel Lewis/Lonely Planet Images: 60 • Sara-Jane Cleland/Lonely Planet Images: 76 • STR/AFP/Getty Images: 56 • Tom Cockrem/Lonely Planet Images: 61, 71, 93 • Ulet Ifansasti/Getty Images: 55 • Wayne Walton/Lonely Planet Images: 96

PRECEDING PAGE
Two girls in traditional dress in a rice field.

Publisher (U.S.): Michelle Bisson
Writers: Gouri Mirpuri, Robert Cooper, and Michael Spilling
Editors: Deborah Grahame-Smith, Stephanie Pee
Copyreader: Tara Tomczyk
Designers: Nancy Sabato, Steven Tan
Cover picture researcher: Tracey Engel
Picture researcher: Joshua Ang

Marshall Cavendish Benchmark
99 White Plains Road
Tarrytown, NY 10591
Website: www.marshallcavendish.us

Originated and designed by Times Media Private Limited
An imprint of Marshall Cavendish International (Asia) Private Limited
A member of Times Publishing Limited

Marshall Cavendish is a trademark of Times Publishing Limited.

Library of Congress Cataloging-in-Publication Data
Mirpuri, Gouri, 1960-
  Indonesia / Gouri Mirpuri, Robert Cooper, Michael Spilling. — 3rd ed.
    p. cm. — (Cultures of the world)
  Summary: "Provides comprehensive information on the geography, history, wildlife, governmental structure, economy, cultural diversity, peoples, religion, and culture of Indonesia"—Provided by publisher.
  Includes bibliographical references and index.
  ISBN 978-1-60870-783-6 (print)
  1. Indonesia—Juvenile literature. I. Cooper, Robert, 1945 Aug. 2- II. Spilling, Michael. III. Title. IV. Series.

DS615.M54 2012
959.8—dc22   2011004463

Printed in Malaysia
7 6 5 4 3 2 1

CONTENTS

INDONESIA TODAY

INDONESIA IS TRULY ONE OF THE MOST DIVERSE COUNTRIES IN THE world, with a landscape, culture, and ethnic mix rarely matched elsewhere. Made up of more than 17,000 islands that sprawl along the equator from the Indian Ocean to the Pacific, the modern Indonesian identity we see today has developed almost as an accident of history. Situated on the key trade route between India and China, the world's largest archipelagic state straddles a massive area between Asia and Australia, and consequently reflects influences from the great civilizations of Asia as well as Europe.

The sheer variety of the many islands and peoples that make up the country cannot be exaggerated enough: Modern Indonesia is a human mosaic of colorful complexity, with around 300 different ethnic groups speaking up to 700 distinct languages and dialects. With a population of around 240 million people, it is the world's fourth most populous country, and is home to the world's largest Muslim population. Although Islam is the dominant religion, Indonesia is not an Islamic country, and tolerates a wide range of religious beliefs, including Christianity, Buddhism, and Hinduism. Although at times religious and ethnic tensions have

Balinese dancers performing a sacred dance.

risen to the surface, Indonesians live in relative harmony and have developed a distinct Indonesian identity since becoming an independent republic in 1949. With its multi-party democracy and free elections, modern Indonesia is a much more politically mature and tolerant place than it was in the Suharto era (1966—98), when authoritarian one-party rule held sway. Today Indonesia has become an example of how a developing country can embrace democracy and diversity, as U.S. President Barack Obama noted in his visit to the country in November 2010.

How did this sprawling archipelago become a single, unified state? Modern Indonesia reflects the parameters of the Dutch colonial administration of the Netherlands East Indies—an area that was steadily brought under Dutch influence from the early 1600s until independence three and half centuries later. Starting with the Spice Islands of Maluku, Dutch rule spread throughout the islands, bringing together this patchwork of different peoples under a single colonial government. From this single territory a unified Indonesian identity emerged that endures to this day. That this artificial creation has survived and prospered is one of the greatest achievements since independence and a testament to the tolerance and civility of the Indonesian people. Differences remain, of course, with people actively campaigning for independence in Papua and Aceh. Groups in Aceh in particular have fought a war of independence for decades. Indonesia's physical and ethnic diversity means that the country does not have a clearly defined, homogeneous cultural identity.

Indonesia's diversity does not just apply to its peoples, but also to its physical environment. The 17,500 islands are home to 40,000 species of plants and more than 600 animal species, as well as 33 998.95 miles (54,716 kilometers) of coastline and numerous volcanoes, 150 of which are known to be active. Many visitors are awed by the spectacular natural landscape, including popular sites such as the lake and volcano at Mount Bromo, the paddy fields of Bali, the dive sites of Lombok and Maluku, and the incredible range of wildlife found throughout the Nusa Tenggara islands.

Indonesia is situated in a very earthquake-prone area, with the highly populated islands of Sumatra and Java home to dozens of active volcanoes.

Volcanic ash being released by one of Indonesia's active volcanoes.

Indonesia was devastated by a tsunami in 2004, More than 160,000 people perished in the disaster.

Across the entire archipelago, more than 40 major earthquakes have been recorded since the year 2000. This includes undersea volcanoes erupting along almost any part of coastline, from Sumatra in the west to Papua in the east, causing tsunamis, or gigantic tidal waves. The worst of these was the massive Indian Ocean tsunami that hit the coast of Sumatra on December 26, 2004, killing upwards of 160,000 Indonesians and destroying many towns and villages in the northwest of the island. Although a tsunami early warning system has been put in place since that terrible catastrophe, the coastal areas of Sumatra and Java live in constant fear of a recurrence.

Visitors to Indonesia discover a friendly and helpful people who are keen to engage with the world outside. Urban Indonesians live much like their counterparts elsewhere, working and spending their leisure time with their friends and family. They might visit the movie theater, watch a *wayang* (WAH-young) or shadow-puppet, performance (especially if they live in rural areas), or go to the night market or shopping mall to shop and eat, enjoying either the deliciously spicy local food, or perhaps Western-style fast food. Indonesian cities are crowded and the streets are often narrow, with heavy traffic jams commonplace in cities such as Jakarta, Yogyakarta, and Surabaya. Although cars are common in all urban areas, people often travel by the more convenient forms of public transportation, including the *ojek* (motorbike pillion), buses, taxis, and *becak* (BAY-chucks) or three-wheeled rickshaws.

Visitors will also notice massive differences in wealth between the urban rich and poor: Neighborhoods of large houses with expensive cars parked outside and staffed by many servants are often just a short drive away from urban slums, where the poor and homeless scrape together a living. It is not unusual to find beggars at street junctions in any of Indonesia's cities. Many

A *dalang*, or puppeteer, brings his puppets to life during a *wayang kulit* performance.

rural areas do not have running water or electricity, and people often drill wells and pump the water into their own storage tanks for household use. The drainage system is also unreliable, and heavy rains often bring flooding in many towns and cities. However, despite these problems, Indonesians cope.

Although Indonesia is not the most prosperous country in Southeast Asia, the economy has grown steadily in recent years, with massive potential growth from its many natural resources, including oil, gas, and timber. It is also in the exploitation of these natural resources that one of the country's greatest challenges lies. Indonesia is home to large tracts of Southeast Asia's last remaining rain forests. Indonesian forests are also being deforested at an incredibly fast rate that is not sustainable over the long term. This threatens the country's precious wildlife, with species such as the orangutan and Komodo dragon protected in special national parks.

Today the Indonesian government, under the leadership of the popular president Susilo Bambang Yudhoyono, faces the issue of how to manage the development of the country in a way that will bring prosperity to all while preserving one of the world's richest and most distinctive ecosystems.

GEOGRAPHY

The beauty of the sulfur lake at Ijien Plateau in east Java belies the danger of the volcano that lies beneath.

1

NDONESIA IS A NATION OF 17,508 islands stretching over 3,200 miles (5,150 km) between the Indian and Pacific oceans, a distance greater than the width of the United States. Its total land area is 699,450 square miles (1,811,569 square km), almost three times the size of Texas, making it the 16th-largest country in the world.

Because 80 percent of the country's territory is in fact water, Indonesians refer to their country as *Tanah Air Kita* (tah-nah ah-yayr kee-tah), which literally means "Our (Nation of) Land and Water."

An aerial view of just some of the islands of Indonesia.

Indonesia, the largest archipelago in the world, lies along the equator at the crossroads of Asia and Australia. This strategic position has greatly influenced its cultural, social, political, and economic life.

Indonesia's five main islands are Sumatra (which is slightly larger than California), Java (almost the size of New York State), Kalimantan (the southern part of the world's third-largest island, Borneo), Sulawesi (about the size of Great Britain), and Irian Jaya (the western portion of the world's second-largest island, New Guinea).

Only 6,670 of Indonesia's islands are inhabited. These vary in size from rocky outcrops to larger islands, but many are so small that they do not even have a name.

GEOLOGICAL HISTORY

The Indonesian islands were formed during the Miocene period, about 15 million years ago, seemingly a long, long time ago but only yesterday on the geological timescale. Most of Indonesia's volcanoes are part of the Sunda arc, which is a 1,864-mile-long (3,000-km-long) line of volcanoes extending from northern Sumatra to the Banda Sea. Most of these volcanoes are the result of the Australia Plate slipping beneath the Eurasia Plate, in a process called subduction.

Indonesia is located in one of the most volatile geological regions in the world. The mountainous spine, which runs right through the archipelago, contains hundreds of volcanoes, of which at least 150 are still active, with 76 recorded eruptions. Wherever you go in Indonesia, you are unlikely to lose sight of the region's huge, conical-shaped mountains, which often have smoke billowing from them. Located on the Pacific Ocean's "Ring of Fire," Indonesia experiences about three tremors a day and at least one volcanic eruption a year.

The ash and debris regularly spewed out by the volcanoes are washed down and deposited in the plains. This whitish ash deposit is so rich in chemicals that it has produced some of the most fertile soils in the world. It has been said that one can push a stick in the ground and it will soon sprout leaves! Three rice crops can be produced in a year without the use of fertilizers, providing the staple food for one of the most populous countries in the world.

RING OF FIRE

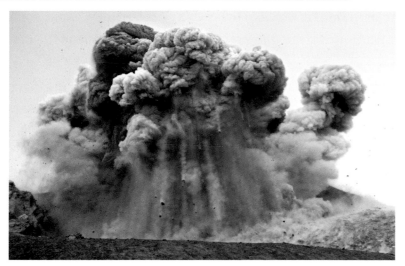

Located where the Sunda and Australian tectonic plates meet, the islands of Sumatra, Java, Bali, Lombok, Flores, and Sumbawa remain forever vulnerable to the destructive effects of earthquakes. A mere 18 months after the catastrophe of the December 26, 2004, tsunami, another major earthquake occurred on May 27, 2006, just 15 miles (25 km) off the southern coast of central Java, one of Indonesia's most densely populated areas. The eruption happened 6 miles (10 km) below the seabed, recording a magnitude of 6.3 on seismographs.

The quake caused terrible devastation in central Java, killing an estimated 5,782 people, injuring more than 36,000, and leaving an estimated 1.5 million people homeless. Tens of thousands of buildings were damaged, mostly homes constructed from low-quality building materials. The ancient Hindu temple complex of Prambanan, one of Indonesia's great historical and architectural treasures, was also severely damaged. Indonesians feared another tsunami, and roads in central Java were crammed with people fleeing the cities of Yogyakarta and Solo. Fortunately the massive destructive waves failed to materialize.

The suffering of the people of Java, however, was to continue. Yet another earthquake occurred on July 17 of the same year. The epicenter of the quake was 222 miles (357 km) south of the capital Jakarta, in the middle of the Indian Ocean. The earthquake caused a 10-foot-high (3-meter-high) tsunami that destroyed houses on the south coast of Java, killing at least 668 people and leaving at least 65 missing. In some places, waves reached 656 feet (200 m) inland, destroying scores of houses. Cars, motorbikes, and boats were left mangled. The Hawaii-based Pacific Tsunami Warning Center (PTWC) issued a tsunami *alert minutes after the earthquake, warning Indonesia and Australia about a possible local tsunami, but the warning did not allow for an evacuation of the coastal areas before the waves struck.*

Sumatra remains very vulnerable to earthquakes, both on the island itself and from the nearby Indian Ocean. In March 2007 two earthquakes in a two-hour period devastated the area around Lake Singkarak in western Sumatra. Dozens of people were killed and many hundreds were injured in towns across western Sumatra, especially in the provincial capital, Padang. More than 40,000 homes were damaged—many of which were small, flimsily built wooden houses—as well as hundreds of schools, mosques, and other government buildings. The earthquakes were felt as far away as Singapore and Malaysia, where some buildings were evacuated as a precaution.

In September 2007 a series of earthquakes in the Java Trench, an area of sea southwest of Sumatra, led to tsunami warnings being issued across the region. One of the earthquakes was of a magnitude of 8.5, making it the fifth-largest earthquake ever recorded. The tremors lasted several minutes, and caused some buildings in the capital, Jakarta, on the island of Java, to sway. Some buildings collapsed in Bengkulu, on the southern coast of Sumatra, just 80 miles (130 km) from the epicenter of the earthquake. Twenty-one people were killed and 88 were injured.

The tremors were felt as far away as Singapore—which is 430 miles (695 km) from the epicenter—and to the north across Peninsula Malaysia and in southern Thailand. After the first and largest earthquake the PTWC put out an alert for the entire Indian Ocean; four tsunami alerts were eventually issued over a 24-hour period.

Further deadly earthquakes struck Sumatra in September 2009, killing more than a thousand people and injuring many more around the city of Padang. In October 2010 another earthquake off the coast of Sumatra registering a magnitude of 7.5 set off a 10-foot-high (3-m-high) tsunami that killed hundreds of people, especially in the Pagai Islands, west of Sumatra. In November 2010 Mount Merapi in central Java also erupted, killing hundreds of people and causing many tens of thousands to flee their homes.

On August 26 and 27, 1883, the volcanic island of Krakatoa erupted in what was one of the most cataclysmic explosions in history. Imagine an explosion so tremendous that:

• *It blew all 8.8 square miles (23 square km) of the island of Krakatoa away.*

• *It produced a detonation that was heard in Australia, 2,200 miles (3,540 km) away.*

• *It threw out nearly 5 cubic miles (21 cubic km) of rock fragments and ash, which fell over 300,000 square miles (800,000 square km).*

• *A total of 36,417 people were killed (official death toll).*

• *Some 165 villages and towns were destroyed.*

• *A tsunami, reaching a height of 120 feet (37 m), followed it and killed about 36,000 people on the adjacent shores of Java and Sumatra.*

• *A series of tidal waves was triggered, reaching as far away as South America and Hawaii.*

• *It produced an ash cloud that was reported to have reached 50 miles (80 km) high. Fine dust from this cloud caused spectacular sunsets all over the world for the next year.*

• *The cloud blocked out the sun such that it was pitch black for two and a half days in the surrounding regions.*

Although Krakatoa was totally blown apart in the 1883 eruption, continuing volcanic activity caused a growing cone of volcanic ash to emerge above sea level by 1928. Anak Krakatoa, or "Child of Krakatoa," had reached a height of 622 feet (190 m) above sea level by 1973. Seismologists are constantly monitoring this young volcano, while geologists and biologists study the life-forms that have since evolved on this island.

THE WALLACE LINE

In the 1850 a British naturalist named Alfred Russel Wallace who was exploring the region noticed that the Indonesian archipelago appeared to have zones of different flora and fauna. He was especially struck by the existence of clear boundaries within which one could find plants and animals typical of the Asian (or Oriental) mainland, those that were associated with Australia, and another zone that had another category of plants and animals. Although many zoogeographers today no longer consider the Wallace Line a regional boundary, it does represent an abrupt limit of distribution for many major animal groups and types of fauna.

One possible explanation for these boundaries is that during the last Ice Age (10,000 B.C.), sea levels dropped so low that the islands on the Sunda Shelf—Borneo, Sumatra, Java, Bali, and some islands on the Lesser Sunda chain—were joined to the Asian mainland. Thus the islands may have once formed a single land mass that was connected to the mainland. If one looks at a map of the island of New Guinea, it appears to fit neatly into northern Australia like a piece of a jigsaw puzzle. It sits on the Sahul Shelf, which is a northeastern extension of the Australian continental mass. This may be why animals that one associates with Australia, such as tree kangaroos and wallabies, can be found here.

In between the Sunda Shelf and the Sahul Shelf lies the Lesser Sunda region, stretching from Bali in the west to Timor in the east. A unique feature of this region is that it contains animal species that are not found anywhere else in Indonesia. This is because the Lesser Sunda region is separated from the other islands by deep sea trenches that are 24,442 feet (7,450 m) at their deepest. Hence, even when sea levels fell during the last Ice Age, this region remained isolated.

CLIMATE

Since Indonesia straddles the equator, it experiences the typical year-long hot and humid weather pattern of tropical countries. Afternoon thunderstorms are common.

Indonesia has only two seasons, and even these are not extremes. The "dry season" lasts from June to September; the "wet season" is from December to March. During the dry season the islands come under the influence of winds from the southeast. The wet monsoon season brings rain from northeasterly winds, moisture-laden after traveling over the South China Sea.

"Rain" is sometimes too mild a word. During the monsoons such tremendous walls of water explode from the sky that it is like standing under a huge waterfall. Rainfall can occur at any time of the year and it is even wetter in the mountainous areas. In these places it becomes hard to distinguish between the wet and dry seasons—especially in Sumatra and Kalimantan, where it never stops raining!

Temperatures average about 81°F (27°C) and vary only according to altitude. Coastal plains experience temperatures of a tolerable 80°F (27°C), although exposure to the noonday sun can result in bad sunburn. As you go higher, the temperature drops by 2°F (1.1°C) every 656 feet (200 m), resulting in a very pleasant 68°F to 72°F (20°C to 22°C) in the highlands. Many Indonesians frequently escape to the mountains to spend their vacations "cooling off" from the heat of the lowlands. Some unusual contrasts exist. The famous Mandala Mountain (15,423 feet [4,701 m]) in Irian Jaya is snow-capped in spite of being on the equator.

Rain is a common occurence in Indonesia.

FLORA

Most of Indonesia is covered in evergreen equatorial rain forests. However, one is just as likely to find mangrove swamps with their looping aerial

The pitcher plant is a carnivorous plant that traps unsuspecting insects in its "pitcher," slowly digesting them.

roots (in eastern Sumatra) and large tracts of arid savannah grassland (in the Lesser Sunda Islands). At higher altitudes there are alpine meadows with chestnut, laurel, and oak trees that are more commonly found in countries with temperate rather than tropical climates.

The abundant rainfall and high humidity have produced some of the densest forests in the world. These forests are also self-fertilizing because the plants decompose and form rich humus (a kind of fertile ground fungus) very quickly after they die.

Indonesian flora is not only abundant but also exotic and incredibly diverse, with more than 40,000 species recorded to date. About 6,000 species of plants are known to be used directly or indirectly by the people. Indonesia has some of the world's richest timber resources and the largest concentration of tropical hardwood. It has more than 3,000 valuable tree species, including durian, teak, ironwood, rattan, ebony, sandalwood, camphor, clove, and nutmeg. Kalimantan and Java are centers for the timber industry, where meranti and teak grow, respectively.

Among its flowers and plants are some 5,000 species of orchids ranging from the largest of all orchids, the tiger orchid, to the tiny Taeniophyllum, which is edible and used in medical preparation and handicrafts. Also found in Indonesia are exotic plants such as the carnivorous pitcher plant that traps insects in its liquid-filled cup and extracts their nutrients, and the strange parasitic creepers that include the strangler fig, with aerial roots that eventually strangle the tree on which it grows.

ONE OF THE LARGEST FLOWERS IN THE WORLD

Found only in the jungles of south-central Sumatra, the immense Rafflesia arnoldii leads a parasitic existence on plant roots and stems. The plant has no leaves but its bud bursts open every couple of months to reveal five huge dark-red petals with white specks. This is the world's largest bloom, which can measure about 1 yard (0.9 m) across and weigh up to 24 pounds (11 kilograms).

FAUNA

Indonesia boasts an incredible variety of wildlife. It is home to 12 percent of the world's mammal species, 16 percent of the world's amphibian and reptile species, 17 percent of the world's bird species, and 25 percent of the world's species of fish.

Its birds and animals include the one-horned rhinoceros of Java; the brilliantly colored bird of paradise, which cannot fly; the tiny Lesser mouse deer, which stands one foot (30 centimeters) tall; the ancient Komodo dragon; the Bali starling with silky snow-white feathers, black wings and tail tips; tigers, tapirs, marsupials such as bandicoots and cuscuses; peacocks, kuau, anoa, and numerous other animals.

Many animal species can only be found in one region and have become extremely rare. The remaining single-horned Sumatran rhinoceros are confined to the Kulon Peninsula National Park in Java. Another endangered species is the orangutan from Borneo and Sumatra. Orangutan rehabilitation

THE LARGEST LIZARD IN THE WORLD

Although dinosaurs are extinct, their latter-day relatives, the fierce Komodo dragons (Varanus komodoensis), have survived for millions of years in Indonesia, on the islands of Komodo and Rinca. These huge lizards can measure up to 10 feet (3 m) long and weigh 150 pounds (70 kg). They take around three to five years to mature, and may live as long as 50 years. They have long scaly bodies supported on short muscular legs, massive tails, and razor-sharp teeth. They eat smaller members of their own kind and occasionally attack and kill human beings, but they mainly feed on carrion. Historians believe that the mythological Chinese dragon may have been fashioned after this creature, whose long, forked, blazing orange tongue seemed to resemble fire.

Almost extinct because of collectors and game hunters, the Komodo dragon soon became a threatened species. In 1980 the Komodo National Park was founded to protect the Komodo dragon populations on the islands of Komodo, Rinca, and Padar, and later the Wae Wuul and Wolo Tado Reserves were established on Flores. Today there are approximately 4,000—5,000 living Komodo dragons in the wild, on the islands of Gili Motang (100), Gili Dasami (100), Rinca (1,300), Komodo (1,700), and Flores (2,000).

centers have been set up at Mount Leuser National Park in northern Sumatra, and in a game preserve in southern Kalimantan. Other endangered animals in Indonesia include the siamang (gibbon), Javan rhinoceros, banteng cattle, Malay tapir, tiger, sun bear, leopard, and elephant.

Indonesia's insect kingdom is just as fascinating, including giant walking sticks that can grow as long as 8 inches (20 cm), walking leaves, huge atlas beetles, and lovely luna moths.

Indonesia has over 50,000 miles (80,467 km) of coastline that make up an extremely diverse and rich environment for coastal plants, animals, and marine life. Indonesia's complex coral reefs and marine ecosystems boast rich sea life, ranging from big game fish—such as marlins, tuna, barracuda, and wahoo—to whales, hammerhead sharks, and manta rays.

INTERNET LINKS

www.volcano.si.edu/world/region.cfm?rnum=06&rpage=list

This website describes all the known active volcanoes in Indonesia, and includes photographs of many of them.

www.komodonationalpark.org/

The official website of the Komodo National Park includes pictures and descriptions of the wildlife found there.

www.indonesia.travel/en/destination/248

Indonesia's official tourism website includes many photographs of the country's wildlife and landscape and links for visitors.

www.photovolcanica.com/VolcanoInfo/Krakatau/Krakatau.html

This site introduces Krakatau (or Krakatoa as it is also known) as it is today, with a description of the volcano's current activity and illustrations and photographs showing how the volcano functions.

HISTORY

Stupas at the Borobudur temple complex. Architecture at this World Heritage site dates back to the eighth and ninth centuries.

2

P REHISTORIC REMAINS DISCOVERED in Indonesia show that one of the earliest humans lived in Java. Fossils of the famous prehistoric "Java Man" were discovered in 1891, and date back some 500,000 years.

HISTORIC MIGRATIONS

The first modern people in Indonesia were dark-skinned, wooly-haired, pygmy Negritos, who arrived about 30,000 to 40,000 years ago, probably from Polynesia. They were followed centuries later by the Australoids, who were also dark-skinned and wooly-haired but had broad, flat noses. Between 3,000 and 500 B.C., both these groups were driven into the highlands and jungles by the migration of Asian peoples from the northern Indochina region: the Proto-Malays and the Deutero-Malays.

The Proto-Malays, from whom today's Bataks and Dayaks are descended, brought with them a Neolithic, or New Stone Age, technology. Settling in the Malay Peninsula and Sumatra, they lived in village settlements, domesticated animals, and cultivated crops. Remnants of their culture can be seen today in the megaliths found in Sumatra. The Deutero-Malays were a second wave of migrants from the Asian mainland who moved south around 300 B.C.

Right: A Papuan mummy discovered in Papua, Indonesia, is an indication that humans had settled in Indonesia a long time ago.

The Candi Sewu temple in Central Java is the second-largest Buddhist complex after Borobudur. It is believed to have originally been named Manjusrigrha.

THE HINDU-BUDDHIST KINGDOMS

Of all the foreign influences at work in Indonesia, the greatest impact was made by Indian culture and religion. In the first to fifth centuries A.D., the Indonesian ruling class, impressed with India's philosophical, religious, and cultural superiority, started to "Indianize" their own kingdoms. They invited Brahmin (members of the priest caste in Indian society) scholars to their courts; sent students to study in India; learned about astronomy and navigational techniques, figure sculpturing, and textile dyeing; adopted numerous Sanskrit words; introduced spices such as cardamom and turmeric into their food; domesticated horses and elephants; and adopted new architectural styles.

The two biggest changes were in the new social status of the rulers and in religion. The Indonesian aristocracy found that they could control their kingdoms better once they introduced the Indian concept of a divine ruler with limitless powers—a descendant of a mythical figure or a reincarnation of the Hindu god Vishnu himself.

India's twin religions—Hinduism and Buddhism—began a peaceful coexistence in Java and Sumatra. Over a period of 1,000 years, Indonesia's history is that of the rise and fall of many Hindu and Buddhist kingdoms. By about the eighth century there were two kingdoms: the Buddhist Srivijaya kingdom in Sumatra, which ruled the seas and major marine routes for the next 600 years, and the Hindu-Buddhist Mataram and Sailendra kingdoms of central Java, which controlled inland rice production for a shorter period of time. In fact Sumatra was called *Swarna Dwipa*, or "Island of Gold," while Java was called *Java Dwipa*, or "Island of Rice." The Srivijaya kingdom was based on foreign trade and controlled the strategic Strait of Malacca. From here spices, incense, and other rare goods were traded between China and India.

The Javanese Mataram and Sailendra kingdoms were more spiritually oriented. The rich soils and wet-rice agriculture supported a huge population, much of which was later employed for the building of the magnificent Borobudur and Prambanan temples. This peaceful coexistence of Hindus and Buddhists did not last long; after a turbulent 300 years or so, there emerged a powerful new Hindu kingdom in Java called the Majapahit. Established in 1293 in an area known for its *pahit* (PAH-hit), meaning "bitter," fruit called *maja* (MAH-jah) this empire marked the golden age of Indonesian history. The Majapahit Empire united the whole of Indonesia and parts of the Malay Peninsula, and ruled for two centuries. It was then that a unique Javanese art and culture developed and flourished.

Around the 14th century this great kingdom went into decline and was invaded by the new Islamic state of Demak. The entire Hindu-Javanese aristocracy fled to Bali, leaving behind a rich Indian-Indonesian heritage.

THE COMING OF ISLAM

When Marco Polo visited Indonesia in 1292, he noted that Islam was already established in parts of Aceh in north Sumatra. The religion was brought by Indian traders plying the India-China trade route.

From Aceh, Islam spread to the rest of the Indonesian archipelago along the trade routes and the paths of economic expansion. To help spread the religion, rulers placed the royal *gamelan* (GAH-may-lahn) orchestras in meeting halls that were turned into mosques. People from the surrounding areas came to listen to the music and were converted in the process. By the 15th and 16th centuries many Indonesian rulers had made Islam the state religion, persuaded by the desire to strengthen ties with the neighboring port of Malacca (modern-day Melaka) on the Malay Peninsula, which had become a center of Islam and trade. The growing international Islamic trade network brought yet more power and wealth. Islam was also a more egalitarian religion than Hinduism. In calling for the equality of all men before God, it had great appeal to the common people.

In the 16th century the Islamic kingdom of Demak attacked the weakening Hindu Mataram kingdom in central Java, taking control of its rich lands and

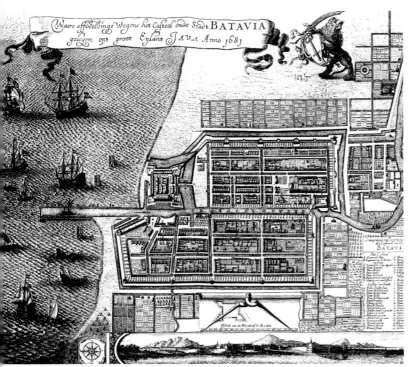

An engraving of Jakarta in 1681, during Dutch colonial rule.

driving the Hindu elite east to Bali. The fall of this once-great empire was recorded by Javanese court chroniclers as "the disappearance of the light of the universe."

THE EUROPEANS

Attracted by the spices of the Far East, the Portuguese found their way to the spice islands of the Moluccas (modern-day Maluku) in 1512 and established trading posts soon after. Their profits encouraged other European traders to come to the region. While the Spanish colonized the Philippines, the Dutch competed for control of the spice trade with the English in the Indonesia archipelago.

In 1596 four Dutch ships arrived at Banten in Maluku after a difficult 14-month voyage during which more than half the crew members died. The few spices they took back to Europe caused so much excitement that, over the next 10 years, 65 more Dutch ships came to the region in search of spices.

The Dutch soon established a strong foothold in Jayakarta (modern Jakarta), which they renamed Batavia. They started sinking the ships of any other country found in Indonesian waters, forcibly took over the spice islands of Banda, and, after more bitter and bloody fighting, gained control of the clove-producing Celebes Island, known as Sulawesi today.

By the end of the 17th century the Dutch controlled not only the spice trade but also monopolized the production of coffee, sugar, indigo, pepper, tea, and cotton on several islands. The powerful Dutch East India Company (*Vereenigde Oost-Indische Compagnie* or VOC) was established to manage this trade and made huge profits from it. Headquartered in Batavia it employed a large army and many servants.

In the 17th and 18th centuries the Dutch expanded their control over the entire Indonesian archipelago, which became known as the Dutch East Indies. On the island of Java peasants were forced to grow export crops, making large profits for the VOC. This domination was achieved at great military expense, however, due to the constant resistance of the local people. This experience finally proved too costly. By 1799 the VOC went bankrupt in what was perhaps the largest commercial collapse in Indonesian history.

For a short time between 1811 and 1815, during the Napoleonic Wars in Europe, the Dutch East Indies territory came under British rule, but then reverted to Dutch rule.

THE NATIONALIST MOVEMENT

The Dutch did little to educate the Indonesians. Ninety percent of the local population was not educated at all. By the 1920s a handful of colleges were opened, and some Indonesians were sent to Holland to be educated. When these scholars returned, they began agitating for freedom.

Two of Indonesia's important national heroes were Diponegoro and Raden Ajeng Kartini. In the early 19th century, Diponegoro, a very popular Javanese prince, fought a guerrilla battle against the Dutch for five years between 1825 and 1830, which cost 200,000 Javanese and 8,000 European lives, mostly through starvation and cholera. Luring him with the bait of negotiations, the Dutch eventually arrested and exiled him in 1830, thus crushing the resistance.

Raden Adjeng Kartini (1879—1904) was less fiery but equally admired. The daughter of a Javanese aristocrat, she was given the opportunity to attend a Dutch school. She was concerned by the impact of colonial rule and the denial of higher education to Indonesians, and by the limited roles available for Indonesian women. In the early 1900s she wrote a series of powerful letters to her Dutch friends in Holland that, when published, caused a stir in the foreign community.

In 1927 the Indonesia National Party (the *Partai Nasional Indonesia* or PNI) was formed under the leadership of a former engineer named Sukarno;

it demanded independence from the Dutch. Sukarno was a gifted speaker and charismatic leader. He became so powerful that he was soon arrested and exiled. At this time the concept of an Indonesian nation was proclaimed in the famous Youth Pledge of 1928: "One People, One Language, One Nation."

JAPANESE OCCUPATION

Independence still seemed a long way off. When the Japanese invaded and occupied the country during World War II, the Indonesians, thinking this signified liberation from Dutch oppression, welcomed them with open arms. The Japanese began a ruthless exploitation of the East Indies. During the three and a half years of Japanese occupation, numerous atrocities were committed by the occupying Japanese army, from the use of mass slave labor in the jungles of Burma and Malaya to starvation in Indonesia when the entire rice crop of Java was exported to Japan.

In order to increase their power among the local population, the Japanese sought to stoke anti-colonial sentiments by promoting the Indonesian language, Bahasa Indonesia, as the national language. They also tried to unite the scattered islands by supporting the nationalists. Both these moves backfired. The confidence this gave the people prompted the nationalist leaders, Sukarno and Mohammed Hatta, to declare Indonesia's independence on August 17, 1945, just one week after the second atomic bomb destroyed Nagasaki in Japan.

At the end of World War II, the Dutch tried to regain control of Indonesia. However, by December 1949, after a long and bloody guerrilla war known as the Indonesian National Revolution, in which as many as 100,000 Indonesians may have died, the Indonesians gained independence from Dutch rule.

INDEPENDENT INDONESIA

The years following independence were not easy, with more than 169 parties struggling for power. In 1959 President Sukarno (1901—70), Indonesia's first post-independence leader, declared martial law and established his

"The landing of the Japanese army made the young (Indonesian) men more dynamic. They were in awe of the Japanese. The Japanese had severely dented the glory of the white man's realm both in mainland Asia and throughout the archipelago."
—Pramoedya Ananta Toer, remarking on the effect the Japanese occupation had on the Indonesian movement for independence

Indonesian soldiers performing drills with lances during the Indonesian National Revolution.

policy of "Guided Democracy." During this period of intense nationalism and anti-colonialism, the old colonial powers of the West were blamed for all of Indonesia's woes.

On September 6, 1965, six of the most senior army generals were killed in an attempted coup. The insurgents backed another rival faction in the army and tried to take control, claiming that they were acting against another coup to overthrow Sukarno. However, the uprising was soon put down by Major General Suharto (1921—2008), commander of the army reserve in Jakarta. In official accounts the coup was blamed on the communist *Partai Komunis Indonesia* (PKI). The effects of the coup were devastating throughout Indonesia, where the military, conservative, and right-wing groups used it as a justification to settle scores with communists and left-wing sympathizers throughout the country. The violence was especially bad in Java and Bali. Estimates vary, but somewhere between 500,000 and 1 million were people were killed over the course of 1965—66.

Faith in Sukarno's leadership soon evaporated, and Suharto, now head of the armed forces, was made acting president in March 1967, and formally appointed in 1968. As head of the army Suharto soon stabilized the country.

General Suharto during his inauguration as Head of Government.

Upon his appointment Suharto quickly imposed martial law: The PKI was outlawed and up to a million people were imprisoned. Suharto also broke ties with communist China and the Soviet Union and revised Indonesia's foreign policy to be friendly to Western interests.

Within Indonesia the entire civil service was reorganized and the army became closely involved in the administration of local government and the economy. The economy gradually set out on a path of high growth through policies aimed at controlling foreign investments, boosting oil exports, slowing population growth, and increasing food production. The inflation rate was reduced and the rupiah stabilized. Suharto's economic "New Order" (*Order Baru*) had begun. Aligning with the interests of the West (the United States and Great Britain), Suharto allowed multinational corporations, the World Bank, and the IMF to enter Indonesia, bringing with this new alignment positive and negative effects. This development brought with it benefits for many with a rising standard of living and increase in educational opportunities, but it also brought the negatives often associated with authoritarian regimes such as lack of open discussion, one-way communication (top-down), and increasing censorship. Suharto became known as the Development President.

REFORMASI: A NEW ERA

The economic crisis that hit in 1997 left Indonesia on the edge of bankruptcy. Rising prices led to riots and looting and anti-Chinese sentiments resurfaced. Suharto was re-elected in February 1998 in the face of open opposition. Street demonstrations were met by tanks and bullets. In three days more than 6,000 buildings in Jakarta were damaged and some 1,200 people died. The Chinese minority bore the brunt of the violence. Suharto's ministers called for his resignation and the presidency was vacated on May 21, 1998, ending 32 years of Suharto's rule.

A period of interim rule by Vice President Habibie did not stop the violence, which spread to the outer islands and took on a Muslim-Christian aspect, which was rare in usually tolerant Indonesia. On August 30, 1999, the East Timorese voted for independence in a referendum. Timor finally became independent in 2002. In an attempt to find a new head of state who would appeal to the diverse elements emerging in Indonesia, Abdurrahman Wahid (known as Gus Dur) was elected the fourth president of Indonesia on October 20, 1999. Abdurrahman, a respected Muslim moderate and chairman of the biggest Muslim organization, *Nahdlatul Ulama* (NU), accepted nationalist Megawati Sukarnoputri (Sukarno's daughter) as vice president. This compromise leadership did not please the conservative Muslims in separatist-minded Aceh, where violence continued.

While secessionist groups in Aceh, Maluku, and Irian Jaya campaigned for independence, changes to Indonesia's political landscape led to a breakdown in central control by the military. Embattled president Abdurrahman Wahid was implicated in two financial scandals. After challenges in parliament and demonstrations on the streets following accusations of corruption, Wahid resigned in 2001 and was replaced by his vice president, Megawati Sukarnoputri. In 2004 Sukarnoputri was unseated in free elections after a successful challenge from former general Susilo Bambang Yudhoyono. SBY, as he is popularly known, was re-elected for a second term in 2009. In the meantime the country had to deal with the destruction caused by the worst natural disaster in modern times, the Indian Ocean earthquake and tsunami that killed more than 170,000 people in Sumatra alone.

INDIAN OCEAN TSUNAMI

On December 26, 2004, the worst natural disaster in modern times occurred: Following an undersea earthquake off the west coast of Sumatra, a massive tsunami was unleashed around the Indian Ocean that killed an estimated 230,000 people in 14 countries. Waves of up to 100 feet (30 m) high devastated coastal communities in Indonesia, Thailand, India, and Sri Lanka, and were even felt as far away as East Africa. With a magnitude between 9.1 and 9.3 on the Richter scale, it is the third-largest earthquake recorded on a seismograph (an instrument used to measure movement in the Earth). This megathrust earthquake caused the entire planet to vibrate as much as a quarter of an inch (0.6 cm) and triggered smaller earthquakes as far away as Alaska.

The epicenter of the earthquake was just 100 miles (160 km) off the northwestern coast of Sumatra, in western Indonesia; the province of Aceh, on the northwest Sumatran coast, bore the worst of the devastation. Along with much of Indonesia, Sumatra is prone to earthquakes because it lies at the boundary of two of the Earth's tectonic plates. More than 160,000 people are thought to have died in Sumatra alone, and numerous villages and towns were completely destroyed, swept away by the tidal wave. For example the town of Meulaboh, which had a population of 120,000 before the tsunami, was struck by a series of waves, killing an estimated 40,000 people and destroying most of the city. The United Nations (UN) estimated that more than 600,000 Indonesians were left homeless by the catastrophe.

The Indonesian authorities were initially overwhelmed by what appeared to be an act of God, and were ill-prepared to deal with a humanitarian crisis on such a massive scale. Troops in the region were dispatched to offer help on the ground. Three days of national mourning were declared. The Indonesian government declared that the provincial Acehnese government was totally crippled and shifted all administrative control to the capital Jakarta.

Fortunately international help soon poured in: Because the disaster happened during what is a holiday period for much of the world, the extensive television coverage helped prompt a huge humanitarian response, with people and governments around the world eventually donating $7 billion in aid to the relief effort across the region. The U.S. government quickly pledged $350 million, and also sent ships and aircraft to help with the aid effort.

However, in Sumatra, although aid was soon flown in by international agencies, a lack of trucks and helicopters, and poor local roads meant that the medicines, food, and tents that people needed did not reach the disaster-struck areas quickly.

In the aftermath of the tsunami Indonesia developed an early warning system designed to give coastal residents enough time to flee or seek shelter from an impending tidal wave. By 2009 a system of 39 deep-sea warning buoys connected to satellite communications had been installed in the seas around Indonesia. A tsunami early warning center in Jakarta was also established to monitor conditions, with information continually analyzed so that fast and accurate warnings could be given in case of emergency.

INTERNET LINKS

www.sjsu.edu/faculty/watkins/indonesia1.htm

This website offers a popular account of the Sukarno era of Indonesian history, from the 1930s to the 1960s.

www.borobudur.tv/

This site includes a webcast and many other photographs of the ninth-century Borobudur Buddhist monument in central Java as well as links to other aspects of Java's historic Buddhist culture.

www.newworldencyclopedia.org/entry/Dutch_East_India_Company

This site provides a detailed account of the Dutch East India Company, with photographs and links.

www.gimonca.com/sejarah/sejarah.shtml

This site provides a detailed timeline of Indonesian history from prehistoric times to the present.

GOVERNMENT

The presidential palace of Indonesia.

ALTHOUGH ELECTIONS HAVE BEEN held in Indonesia for many decades under the New Order regime, it is only recently that they have been judged fair and open by outside observers. In July 2009 Susilo Bambang Yudhoyono became the first Indonesian president ever re-elected, winning a landslide victory in democratic elections.

More than 120 million people cast ballots and Yudhoyono captured 61 percent of the vote, winning in 28 of Indonesia's 33 provinces.

THE NATIONAL GOVERNMENT

The Indonesian parliament is made up of two houses. The highest political body is the *Majelis Permusyawaratan Rakyat* (MPR, or People's Consultative Assembly), which elects the president, decides on policies, and issues decrees that have the effect of law. The MPR consists of 695 members, 560 of whom are legislators directly elected by the populace every five years. These legislators also form the *Dewan Perwakilan Rakyat* (DPR or House of Representatives). The others consist of appointed regional delegates and those from different interest groups, such as the army, women's groups, children, sports people, business, and religious groups.

Indonesia is a democratic republic with a presidential system of government. The president is both the head of the government and the head of state.

The national crest and flag of Indonesia.

DPR members belong to the main political parties, which, since the 2009 general election, consist of the Democrat Party (PD), Functional Groups Party (GOLKAR), Indonesia Democratic Party-Struggle (PDI-P), National Awakening Party (PKB), National Mandate Party (PAN), People's Conscience Party (HANURA), Prosperous Justice Party (PKS), and United Development Party (PPP). The Democrat Party is the largest party in the assembly, with 148 seats, followed by the Functional Groups Party, with 106 seats.

The president, who is both head of state and chief executive, is elected to a five-year term. The president can only serve two five-year terms after which he cannot seek reelection. The president appoints a Cabinet to carry out state policy and is responsible to the MPR.

THE REGIONAL LEVEL

Indonesia is divided into 33 provinces, including the three special territories of Jakarta (the capital), Yogyakarta, and Aceh. Each province has a capital and is headed by a governor and its own legislative body. Governors and members of the legislative body are elected every five years by popular

SUSILO BAMBANG YUDHOYONO

Born in Tremas, Pacitan, East Java on September 9, 1949, Yudhoyono served in the army from 1973 to 1999, reaching the rank of general. He held various posts around the Indonesian archipelago, and underwent further training at Fort Benning in the United States. He also studied for a master's degree and PhD, receiving his doctorate in agricultural economics in 2004.

Indonesia's sixth president first took office on October 20, 2004, after successfully finishing ahead in the polls in the second-round run-off election against Megawati Sukarnoputri, the standing president since 2001 and the daughter of one of Indonesia's founding fathers, Sukarno. A part of both President Wahid's and President Megawati's governments, SBY (as he is known) was promoted as the people's candidate, especially after a public falling out with the aristocratic Megawati.

Yudhoyono's manifesto focused on improving the country's economy, built on four main principles: prosperity, peace, justice, and democracy. Yudhoyono has a reputation as a strong communicator who has sought to build a progressive coalition that included all the main parties, the army, and business leaders. Since becoming president Yudhoyono has taken a leading role in battling global warming. In 2007 Indonesia led a New York summit of eight countries that are home to 80 percent of the world's rain forest—Brazil, Cameroon, Congo, Costa Rica, Gabon, Indonesia, Malaysia, and Papua New Guinea.

In his younger days he was also a musician, and since becoming president he has recorded three albums of love ballads and religious songs.

vote. The provinces are further divided into districts, each with a *bupati* (boo-PAH-tee) or regent as its head. Within the districts are hundreds of little towns and villages, headed respectively by the *walikota* (WAH-lee-koh-tah) or mayor and village headmen. The village headman is guided by the village council of elders.

DECISION MAKING

Whether at the topmost level of state or down in the tiny villages, all decisions in Indonesia are made in a similar manner. This is through *musyawarah* (moo-SHU-AH-rah), or consultation, and *mufakat* (moo-FAH-kaht), or agreement, until a consensus is reached. It can be a long and tiring process. The government emphasizes a system of consensus so that everyone agrees with the final result. Although this was the ideal in many circumstances those with more status and power were able to impose

Supporters of the Democrat Party of Indonesia take to the roads to show their support during an election campaign.

NEIGHBORLY RELATIONS

Although the two countries have similar historical and social roots, Indonesia has often had a tense relationship with its neighbor, Malaysia. In the 1960s President Sukarno's policy of Konfrontasi (confrontation) led to some minor border clashes, especially on the Kalimantan—Sarawak border on the island of Borneo. Sukarno's government sought to destabilize the fledgling Malaysian state in an attempt to claim the whole of Borneo as Indonesian territory, which it saw as historically and ethnically a part of the Indonesian archipelago.

In the last 20 years many Indonesians have gone to work in Malaysia, often in unskilled or low-paid jobs such as construction, catering, or as maids (live-in home helpers). The standard of living in Malaysia is higher than that of Indonesia— Malaysia has a population that is roughly 10 percent the size of Indonesia's, and has grown its economy at a faster pace over the last 40 years. Both Malaysia and the wealthy city-state of Singapore have at times received bad press in Indonesia for the alleged abuse of maids, and also for the treatment of Indonesian migrant workers. Although many of the workers were illegal, they were tacitly tolerated by a government that needed cheap labor for construction projects; many have since been deported.

The two countries have also been at loggerheads over disputed claims to the oil-rich waters between the two countries, especially in the Celebes Sea, off the east coast of Borneo. In 2010 Malaysian fishermen were arrested for supposedly fishing in Indonesian waters, while Indonesian fishery inspectors were detained by Malaysian maritime police. Indonesian and Malaysian military craft have often squared up to each in a show of force, but without any actual armed confrontation.

More recently Indonesian nationalists have grown angry at the perceived sense that Malaysia is stealing their neighbor's cultural heritage, after an advertisement on cable television in 2009 featured a traditional Balinese dance promoting Malaysian tourism. Protesters in Jakarta burned the Malaysian flag and called for retaliation from their government. This followed a 2007 dispute, where the Malaysian tourist authority used a folk song that originated in Indonesia's Maluku islands to promote the country to visitors.

Despite the tensions the two countries rely heavily on each other for trade and investment, and a genuine conflict seems unlikely in the foreseeable future. But the old resentments from the days of Konfrontasi *remain.*

their will on the majority; this was especially true during the authoritarian regime of Suharto. In the ideal Indonesian-style democracy everyone's views are heard, considered, and taken into account to reach a solution that is acceptable to all concerned.

Another important system of administration in Indonesia is based on the concept of *gotong royong* (goh-TOHNG roh-YOHNG), where everyone works together to achieve a common goal. The *gotong royong* system means that the entire community has a joint responsibility to cooperate with each of its members. Whether there is a flood, volcanic eruption, or it is just harvest time, everyone in the village volunteers to help a needy neighbor. In this way anyone who is in trouble gets help, and the job gets done much more quickly.

PANCASILA DEMOCRACY

Just as the United States has its Bill of Rights, Indonesia has its *Pancasila*, or Five Principles. Indonesian democracy is based on these principles, and is called Pancasila democracy. These principles, declared by President Sukarno in 1945, are a combination of ideas with a focus on traditional rural customs.

Pancasila now serves as a way of life for Indonesia's millions of people who learn about it in school, when they work for the government, and throughout their lives. In fact the entire first week of the new school term is called "Pancasila Week."

PANCASILA, THE FIVE PRINCIPLES

Today the values of Pancasila constitute the state policy and the life philosophy of all Indonesians. The values of Pancasila represent an ideal toward which Indonesians are encouraged to strive.

1. Belief in one supreme God

Indonesians believe in God and most follow one of four great world religions—Islam, Buddhism, Hinduism, or Christianity.

2. Humanitarian justice

Indonesians do not tolerate oppression, either physical or spiritual.

3. National unity

In 1928 Indonesia's youth pledged to have one country, one nation, and one language, binding together the diverse peoples of the archipelago.

4. Indonesian-style democracy

There is consultation (musyawarah) and mutual assistance (gotong royong) to reach consensus (mufakat). It is also referred to as Pancasila-style democracy.

5. Social justice

There is an equal distribution of welfare and the protection of the weak.

INTERNET LINKS

http://news.bbc.co.uk/1/hi/8315624.stm

This site offers news coverage of Susilo Bambang Yudhoyono's historic presidential win in 2009.

http://topics.nytimes.com/topics/reference/timestopics/people/y/ susilo_bambang_yudhoyono/index.html

This website offers analysis of Susilo Bambang Yudhoyono's win in the presidential race in 2009.

ECONOMY

Fishermen fishing in the surf on Lombok.

NDONESIA IS ONE OF THE WORLD'S major suppliers of rubber and is also a major exporter of petroleum, natural gas, oil, tin, plywood, and textiles. It produces commodities such as coffee, tea, tobacco, copra, spices (cloves and nutmeg), and oil-palm products. Its labor force was 113.7 million in 2009, but most people are still mainly employed in agriculture.

The agricultural products Indonesia produces also include rice, cassava (tapioca), peanuts, cocoa, copra (dried kernel of a coconut), poultry,

4

Despite the recent global recession and financial crisis, the Indonesian economy has grown steadily due to the sound leadership of the Yudhoyono administration.

Tea-pickers in Gunung Lawu. Tea is one of Indonesia's export commodities.

Miners panning for gold in Cempaka, South Kalimantan.

beef, pork, and eggs. Tourism, chemical fertilizers, and food production also contribute to the economy. With some of the world's largest tracts of exploitable forest, Indonesia's timber industry has grown rapidly.

Indonesia made impressive economic progress during the years leading up to the Asian financial crisis in 1997. (Between 1981 and 1997 the economy grew by an average of 6 percent per year.) The economic and financial crisis of 1997 to 1999 had a severe impact on Indonesia, with the currency losing value and the economy in freefall. Growth dropped to zero in 1999 but recovered to about 4 percent in 2000. In recent years the Indonesian economy has grown steadily, due to increased revenues from oil and timber under the sensible guidance of Yudhoyono's government. In 2009 the economy grew by 4.5 percent, following 6 percent growth in 2008 and 2007. This growth occurred despite the worldwide economic and financial crisis between 2008 and 2010, putting Indonesia in a strong position as the world economy recovers during the second decade of the century.

SOURCES OF REVENUE

MINERALS AND ENERGY Indonesia has vast mineral and energy resources. A big money earner is oil and gas, which are both managed by the government. Indonesia produces 1.023 million barrels of oil per day, making it the world's 22nd-largest oil producer. Petroleum refining is carried out by the state oil firm, Pertamina. The government is seeking to replace crude oil exports with exports of refined petroleum products and petrochemicals. In recent years Indonesia's home consumption of oil and gas has increased, meaning that the country has had to import some oil to make up a shortfall in demand.

Indonesia is the world's largest tin market. The country is also rich in coal, iron, copper, bauxite, nickel, lead, gold, silver, manganese, zinc, titanium, and uranium.

INDUSTRY Industrial development has made great strides in Indonesia as a result of diversification to reduce the country's dependence on oil. Investment restrictions have been relaxed, and greater incentives are now offered to foreign investors to set up manufacturing plants in Indonesia. Indonesia has a light manufacturing sector involved in a wide range of products, from producing handicrafts and clothing to assembling foreign cars. It also has cement, fertilizer, timber processing, steel, machinery, and oil-related industries.

An employee checks the machinery at a polyester spinning plant.

AGRICULTURE Indonesia remains a largely agricultural country, with the majority of the population working on the land. Agriculture makes up roughly 15 percent of national gross domestic product (GDP).

Indonesia is one of the world's largest producers of rice. This is due to the fertility of its country's soils, which has been helped by the introduction of high-yielding varieties of rice in 1968. On the inner islands most of the rice is grown on terraced *sawah* (sah-wah) or wet-rice fields, the traditional method of farming for the last 2,000 years.

Palm oil comes from the fruit of the oil-palm tree, a tropical species that originated in West Africa, but now grows in many parts of the world, including Southeast Asia and Central America. Palm oil is used as vegetable oil for cooking, and increasingly as an alternative fuel source. Indonesia produces 44 percent of the world's oil palm, closely followed by neighboring Malaysia (43 percent).

Farmers harvesting rice. Indonesia is one of the largest exporters of rice in the world.

On the outer islands, where the soils are not as rich and there is less population pressure on the dry fields, *ladang* (lah-dahng) and "slash and burn" cultivation is popular. This involves clearing several acres of forest land, using it for planting crops for a couple of years, and then moving on once the soil is depleted. Environmentalists are concerned that this practice does not allow the soil to regain its fertility and leads to fires that rage out of control. The pressure often results from overuse of the land by logging contractors or government resettlement programs, which put more people on the land than can be sustained. The overuse of pesticides by Indonesian farmers has also led to a developing resistance of pests to pesticides and the elimination of natural predators that control these pests.

Indonesia is one of the world's main producers of natural rubber, along with Malaysia and Thailand, and a top producer of cloves and coffee. Other agricultural crops grown are corn, cassava, soybeans, palm oil, tea, spices, and tobacco.

TOURISM Indonesia's travel industry is growing and is an increasingly important part of the economy. In 1999 approximately 5 million tourists

TERROR IN PARADISE

On October 12, 2002, three bombs ripped through the popular resort town of Kuta, Bali, killing 202 people and injuring 240. The attack was the deadliest act of terrorism in Indonesian history. Many of the dead and injured were foreigners (including 88 Australians). The bomb attack was preceded by a blast at the U.S. consulate in the Balinese capital, Denpasar, the same day.

Suspicion for the attack quickly fell upon Jemaah Islamiyah (JI), a Southeast Asian-based terrorist organization that seeks to establish an Islamic state across the region. Formally founded in 1993 the organization has active networks in Indonesia, Malaysia, the Philippines, and Singapore, and has known links with the international terror organization Al-Qaeda. JI has also been blamed for attacks in the past, including a series of church bombings in Indonesia in 2000 and strikes on U.S. targets in the Philippines.

The leader of JI, Islamic cleric Abu Bakar Bashir, was soon arrested. Although he was not charged with the Bali atrocity due to lack of evidence, he was charged and convicted of being involved in another bomb attack against the Marriott Hotel in Jakarta in 2003. Bashir was eventually found guilty of conspiring in the Bali attack, and served a short prison term, being released in late 2006. Three other men were convicted for direct involvement in the bombings, and following the failure of legal appeals, they were executed by firing squad in November 2008.

A permanent memorial to the victims was erected on the site of the pub destroyed by the bombings in Kuta. The economically important tourist industry suffered in the aftermath of the Bali bombing, taking years to recover its place as a leading holiday destination.

visited the country. In 2002 tourism throughout Indonesia was badly affected by the Bali bombings in the tourist town of Kuta, and many visitors stayed away for the next few years because of security fears. However, the number of international tourists bounced back positively in 2007, and reached a new record in 2008, with 6.43 million visitors. In 2009 the number climbed yet higher to 6.45 million arrivals, with tourists spending $6.3 billion.

Bali, Java, and North Sumatra currently draw the most tourists. Visitors go to Bali for the beaches, temples, and cultural sites, while they go to Yogyakarta for ancient monuments such as Borobudur and Prambanan, and to see the palace in the city center. The national parks in Sumatra are popular among wildlife lovers, and divers like to go to Lombok and Maluku for the rich marine life. The government has sought to encourage tourism by constructing new hotels, theaters, and art galleries in cultural centers such as Yogyarkarta and Bali and by promoting the remoter islands—for example by opening an

A local artist paints on a temporary tattoo for a tourist. Indonesia's beautiful beaches attract thousands of tourists a year.

airstrip at Tana Toraja in Sulawesi. Local and foreign entrepreneurs have also cashed in by opening hotels, restaurants, bars, and souvenir shops along seafronts. Tourism has also had a negative effect in many areas, putting a greater strain on local resources and damaging the environment through the pollution of coastal waters.

FISHING AND FORESTRY As one would expect of an island nation, the fishing industry is important to Indonesia. Government efforts to promote this industry have been successful, and shrimp export revenues have become an important foreign exchange earner for Indonesia.

Although depletion in recent years has been alarming, Indonesia has the second-largest forest reserves in the world after the Amazon jungle in South America. These reserves are largely on the islands of Sumatra, Kalimantan (Borneo), and Papua, and are another source of revenue.

INTERNET LINKS

www.360cities.net/image/fishing-village#-3.41,16.47,90.0

This website offers a 360-degree view of a Javanese fishing village close to the capital, Jakarta.

www.indonesia-tourism.com

This site outlines the leisure and entertainment that is on offer to tourists who visit Indonesia, broken down by region and topic.

www.flickr.com/photos/leoroubos/2149104027/

This site provides photographs of tapping rubber in Sumatra.

www.pecad.fas.usda.gov/highlights/2007/12/Indonesia_palmoil/

This article analyzes oil-palm production in Southeast Asia, with handy graphs and diagrams to aid understanding.

ENVIRONMENT

Indonesia is not only renowned for its gorgeous
beaches, but also for breathtaking mountains
and rocky peaks like this.

5

INDONESIA HAS A VARIETY OF habitats and ecosystems rarely equaled in the world. Almost 60 percent of all tropical forests in Asia, and about 90 percent of Asia's virgin forests, are found in Indonesia. This vast country contains mangrove swamps, glaciers in Irian Jaya, coral atolls in the Flores Sea, and dense rain forests in Kalimantan, Sumatra, and Irian Jaya.

Sadly economic growth, massive population increases, and ecological disasters have thrown the environment into disharmony. At the start of

The early morning sun highlights the deep etching of erosion on the slopes of Gunung Kursi in east Java.

Indonesia has one of the most diverse ecosystems in the world, including tropical forests, a rich marine life, and a chain of highly active volcanoes.

the 21st century Indonesia had the dubious distinction of having the greatest number of endangered species in the world, with animals such as the Javan rhinoceros, silvery gibbon, Sumatran orangutan, and the Flores shrew all critically endangered.

Indonesia has one of the largest areas of remaining rain forest in the world, but also one of the highest deforestation rates, second only to Brazil. Deforestation has led to soil erosion in the uplands of provinces such as Java, South Sumatra, Lampung, South Sulawesi, and East Nusa Tenggara. Logging has had a particularly damaging effect on the rain forest in Kalimantan, which in turn has led to soil erosion and affected local wildlife. Urban areas suffer from flooding, and inadequate sewage and waste disposal systems have led to air and water pollution. Many of Indonesia's major fishing grounds have been depleted and the rivers polluted.

The government has taken measures to conserve wildlife and the environment by setting up protected areas and parks, developing ecotourism, and directing programs to clean up water pollution. Foreign conservation groups are also increasingly active in wildlife conservation.

The rain forest canopy of Bukit Bankirai in Kalimantan. Indonesia is in danger of losing its rain forest to deforestation.

AN ENVIRONMENT IN DANGER

In recent years millions of Indonesians migrated from overpopulated areas of intensive rice cultivation, such as Java and Madura, to lightly populated areas that were traditionally used for forestry, especially in Kalimantan and Sumatra. These transmigrants in many cases attempted to re-create the irrigated rice fields that they left behind. In order to create new rice lands, the slower-growing hardwood forests and their particular ecosystems were destroyed by the transmigrant population, as compared to local residents, who sought to manage the resources in a sustainable way. For example, over 3,861 square miles (1 million hectares) of peat forest were drained of water that was originally held in giant natural reservoirs, and animals have been hunted for food and profit to the point where they now provide very little of either.

Vague land ownership laws have allowed individuals and companies to clear land as a way to stake a claim, and laws that regulate the use of fire for land clearing have not been enforced. The short-term lease of forest land

A farmer prepares the ground for a new crop. Many farmers practice slash-and-burn cultivation, where all vegetation on their plot of land is cleared and then burned. The subsequent ash then acts as fertilizer for the new crop.

to timber companies provides the exploiters with no incentive to manage the forests in a sustainable manner. The result has been the denudation of forests and an irresponsible use of fire. This combustible combination has resulted in large-scale forest fires that occur with alarming and increasing frequency.

THE DOLLAR FOREST

Almost half of Indonesia is forested, making up an area of 341,681 square miles (884,950 square km). For thousands of years the forest provided Indonesians with building materials, food, clean water sources, and fertile soil for small-scale cultivation. During all this time it did not carry a price tag. Now it does.

Logging for tropical timbers and pulpwood is the main cause of forest loss, although increasingly large tracts of land have been cleared to make way for oil-palm plantations. Indonesia is the world's largest exporter of

Precious trees logged for fuelwood. If this practice goes unchecked, Indonesia stands to lose not only its forests but also the ecosystem and wildlife that live within them.

tropical timber, generating more $5 billion every year. Palm oil plantations generate a further $10 billion. More than 185,329 square miles (480,000 square km) (55 percent of the country's remaining forests) have been leased to logging concessions. The size of the rain forest has steadily declined since the 1960s when 82 percent of the country was covered with forest, to 68 percent in 1982, to 53 percent in 1995, and 49 percent today. Much of the logging is carried out illegally, with some timber groups moving into more remote locations in Kalimantan and Irian Jaya, cutting deeper and deeper into the jungle to find suitable trees. For example, in the mid-1990s, only 7 percent of Indonesia's logging concessions were located in Irian Jaya, but today more than 20 percent exist in the territory.

An aerial view of a timber logging plant.

Kalimantan is home to almost 10 percent of the world's tropical rain forest as well as a remarkable biodiversity that continually multiplies, with three new species being discovered there on average every month. Environmentalists claim that the logging in Kalimantan in particular has contributed to global climate change on a scale that far outweighs the island's size. When the larger trees are cut down by loggers, the effect on the rest of the forest is huge, with the smaller trees nearby dying, too, and the soil becoming loosened and eroded. This in turn allows a free flow of flood waters that drowns more trees, loosens the soil further, and destroys the habitat of all the local wildlife. The orangutan population of Borneo is particularly threatened, and some experts estimate that these apes could be extinct in Borneo within 10 years if deforestation continues at its current rate.

FOREST ON FIRE

With increasing frequency Indonesia's forests in Sumatra and Kalimantan have become victims of fires raging out of control. In 1983 some 13,510 square miles (35,000 square km) of forest were destroyed in Kalimantan. This was followed by fires that lasted for months in both Sumatra and Kalimantan in 1991, 1994, and most notably in 1997, which was reported as the greatest ecological disaster the world had ever seen. Nearby Singapore and Malaysia lived for months under the pollution of the "great haze" and complained that Indonesia had not done enough to prevent or control its fires. Further forest fires on Sumatra in October 2010 also caused alarm in Singapore and Malaysia, as a smoky haze developed above the island city-state and the Malaysian capital Kuala Lumpur.

The tragedy is that these fires were largely preventable. The moist conditions and dense hardwoods found in a tropical rain forest do not burn easily. Only when the forests are degraded and thinned of their natural cover do they readily catch the flames from fires set by farmers burning their fields in preparation for the annual agricultural cycle.

The financial damage from the 1997 fires was estimated at $4.5 billion. This wiped out the export earnings from forest products for one year. It also

A firefighter puts out a small forest fire. Many farmers practice slash-and-burn cultivation and fires that spiral out of control can often rage into uncontrollable forest fires.

THE IRREPLACEABLE RATTAN

Indonesia's lucrative rattan industry accounts for some 90 percent of the world's rattan trade. Exploitation of this plant has increased dramatically in Indonesia, however, as supplies in neighboring Malaysia and Thailand dry up.

There are more than 300 species of rattan palm in Indonesia, but rattan—and its mini-ecosystem of martial ants, bees, wasps, and beetles—is yet another Indonesian plant that is in danger of eventual extinction.

The thorny rattans are climbing palms that need tall trees for support. Their seeds, only one per fruit, take up to six months to germinate on the shaded forest floor and require moist forest soil and a complex interaction of insects, fungi, and bacteria to survive. Indonesia's forest peoples eat the "hearts" of the rattans (the bunch of folded young leaves at the center of the plant) and extract red dye from the fruits. In addition to being made into furniture, rattan is widely used for basket-weaving, walking sticks, fish traps, and suitcases.

made an incalculable contribution to global warming and human suffering in Indonesia and its neighboring countries.

WHAT IS BEING DONE?

The Indonesian government set up a ministry dedicated to the environment in 1993—the Ministry for the Environment. This ministry led programs to control pollution, such as the Clean River Program or Program Kali Bersih (PROKASIH), and the replanting of trees. Protected wildlife parks and areas were also set up.

The World Wildlife Fund (WWF) established itself in Indonesia in 1962 and greatly expanded its activities in the early decades of the 21st century. Its aim

Orangutans are quiet, gentle primates who spend most of their lives in trees. Their name, orangutan, means "man of the forest." Recent scientific analysis of DNA confirms that the orangutan is one of the human's closest relatives. Outside of the world's zoos, orangutans exist only on the Indonesian islands of Borneo and Sumatra. To survive in their natural state, orangutans require large expanses of primary forest. Over-farming of rattan has removed much of the orangutan's habitat, and the great forest fires of the last 20 years have added to their plight. The orangutan is considered critically endangered by the International Union for Conservation of Nature (IUCN), with the population in Sumatra being estimated at around 7,000 and falling fast.

In addition to rattan and other palms, orangutans eat sweet pulpy fruits, insects, young leaves, sap, honey, and mushrooms. Fires and forest exploitation patterns have disturbed the ecosystems that provide this diet. Orangutans have coped with hunger by migration and dietary change: stripping bark from trees to eat the softer interior. Reduction of fruit in their diet has led to a reduction in fertility.

Orangutans suffer an additional threat caused by their resemblance to humans and the human desire to possess the cute and cuddly. Females are often shot in order to obtain their babies, which are sold as pets. Orangutans raised in captivity pick up a range of human diseases and, if released, they carry these to other orangutans in the forest.

is to preserve what remains and to reverse the damage to the environment. On behalf of the government it prepared the Indonesian National Biodiversity Action Plan in 1991 and in 1995 signed a cooperation agreement with the

Ministry of Environment. The WWF has 20 major projects throughout Indonesia. It was instrumental in expanding the national park network and nature reserves. There are now national laws governing the clearing of land by fire, logging, harvesting, and hunting or collecting animals and plants. It is hard to enforce such laws, however, and Indonesia's political and economic problems have tended to take priority over conservation problems. The WWF now works closely with farming communities and industry in an attempt to introduce a "culture of conservation."

The role of environmental non-government organizations (NGOs) is expanding rapidly under the Yudhoyono government. Other than the WWF the local and foreign NGOs include the Indonesian Forum for the Environment (*Wahana Lingkungan Hidup Indonesia*, or WALHI) and the Leadership for Sustainable Development Foundation (*Yayasan Pembangunan Berkelanjutan*, or LEAD Indonesia). Research and development centers have also come to play an important role in environmental management.

INTERNET LINKS

http://walrus.wr.usgs.gov/tsunami/sumatraEQ/SumatraNW1pic.html

This website has a movie graphic showing the movement and extent of the Indian Ocean tsunami shortly after the undersea earthquake in December 2004.

http://rainforests.mongabay.com/20indonesia.htm

This site offers detailed coverage and data on Indonesia's environmental issues, including the effects of timber logging and farming methods on the rain forest.

www.animalinfo.org/country/indones.htm

Based on the 2004 IUCN Red List of Threatened Animals, this site catalogs the many dozens of threatened and endangered species that live in Indonesia.

In 2010 a spokesperson for WALHI claimed that 300 community forest programs developed by local people had lost in their struggle to stop their land and forests being converted into oil-palm plantations.

INDONESIANS

A woman balances a basket on her head as she walks along the street with her daughter.

INDONESIA IS THE FOURTH MOST populated country in the world—after China, India, and the United States—and its population was estimated in 2010 at 242 million.

6

Indonesia has a large population of diverse peoples spread across many islands.

POPULATION PRESSURES

The population distribution from island to island is uneven. More than 136 million people, some 57 percent of the entire population, live on Java, although the island accounts for only 7 percent of the total land area of Indonesia. With more than 2,500 people crammed into every square mile (1,000 people per square km), Java is the world's most densely populated agricultural land. In recent years many people have moved to the large cities of West Java, such as the capital Jakarta, for work. West Java's population growth rate remains the highest among all provinces in Java. At 20 percent it is much higher than the growth rate of Central Java (3 percent), East Java (7 percent), and Yogyakarta (12 percent). In contrast Kalimantan, which accounts for over 25 percent of Indonesia's land area, is home to only 10.4 million people, or 5 percent of the population. Bali and Madura also have high population densities.

Right: A family in Belakang Padang.

A family living in a rural area. Most of Indonesia's population lives in rural areas.

About 70 percent of Indonesians live in rural areas. In fact Indonesia has been called a nation of villages, having more than 60,000. However, Indonesia also has some of the largest cities in Asia. In 2010 Jakarta's population was 9.6 million. As Jakarta continues to grow, it is merging with the surrounding towns. Local authorities have set themselves the target of limiting the population of Jakarta to 12 million, believing that anything larger will lead to massive social problems, with public services and infrastructure being stretched to the breaking point.

Indonesia has a young population, with about one-third of the people under 20 years of age. This is due to the high population growth rate, especially among the poorer sections of society, where people have many children as insurance for themselves in their old age. The average life expectancy is 70 years. By 2020, however, the number of Indonesians aged 60 years and above is projected to reach 11.4 percent of the total population—a future problem for policymakers.

Indonesia's population problems have been dealt with in two ways: by controlling growth through family planning and by spreading distribution through a transmigration program. Its success in increasing the use of contraceptives is good news given the fact that Indonesia's labor force is also growing, including women of childbearing age. The transmigration program, however, has not been successful, with migrants rarely settling into their new environment or finding acceptance from the local inhabitants.

ETHNIC HISTORY

One of the most fascinating features of Indonesia is the incredible diversity of its people. It is a country where more than 300 different ethnic groups speak 250 distinct languages and have their own individual culture and

TWO IS ENOUGH

Population pressure is a problem in overcrowded Java and Bali. In these densely populated areas farmers struggle to make a living from tiny plots of land. In the urban centers the situation is worse, as millions are crammed into tiny shacks in congested slums along narrow back alleys.

To combat its population crisis, Indonesia has launched a family planning campaign. "Two Is Enough" is the motto of the active National Family Planning Coordinating Board. The success of the program can be measured by the fact that 21.3 million couples were practicing some form of family planning by 1993, compared with only 400,000 in 1972. In 2006 it was estimated that without the family planning program, the country's population probably would have reached 280 million by 2010—40 million more people than the actual population. One factor that has helped is that there is no preference for boys, unlike in countries such as China and India. Family planning has become such an open topic in Indonesia that in the villages "King and Queen of Contraception" contests are held! In the cities it is perfectly normal to ask people what contraceptive method they use.

Transmigration has also been introduced to ease population pressures. First introduced by the Dutch in 1904, the scheme was expanded under President Suharto. It involves moving people from the densely populated areas of Java, Bali, and Madura to the more thinly populated areas of Kalimantan, Papua, and Sumatra. At the program's peak between 1979 and 1984, almost 2.5 million people were moved. The government claims to offer this program voluntarily. Those who are moved are usually the poorest families from urban and rural areas. Once they reach their new homes, they are given 5 acres (2 ha) of land, a house, one year's supply of food, basic farming tools, and seeds to start life afresh. However, in recent years the program has been scaled back, partly because of a lack of government funds and partly because of tensions and occasional violence between the migrants and the local populations, especially in Kalimantan. Migrants often lack understanding of their new environment and local resources, and have sometimes been guilty of carrying out unsustainable farming practices.

customs. This is a land where four of the world's major religions are practiced—Islam, Hinduism, Buddhism, and Christianity. Even the physical appearance of the people varies from region to region. They differ vastly in skin and hair coloring, hair type, and facial features.

There are two theories about how such a diverse group of people populated the Indonesian archipelago. One theory suggests that large groups of people migrated in waves to Indonesia over several centuries from the Asian mainland. The other theory is that there was no coordinated mass movement; instead the various races that came to Indonesia did so in small groups, mixed and mingled with the local people, and, over several centuries, replaced the original inhabitants.

It appears that at least four distinct groups have migrated to Indonesia over the centuries: the Negritos, the Australoids, the Proto-Malays, and the Deutero-Malays. This migration must have been relatively easy because during the last Ice Age, the sea level was low enough for the islands of the Sunda Shelf to be linked to mainland Southeast Asia.

The Chinese are among Indonesia's most recent immigrants. Many people moved to the archipelago in the late 19th and early 20th century to trade. Although they are a tiny minority, they are an important part of society and control a large portion of Indonesia's wealth.

ETHNIC GROUPS

In this country of scattered islands, high mountains, and dense jungle, it is the sea that unites and the land that divides. Thus it is common to find similarities among peoples on adjoining islands but differences between the peoples of coastal and interior regions. Although Indonesians have local ethnic identities, marriages between, say, people from Java and Sumatra are common, and ethnic Chinese Indonesians often marry non-Chinese Indonesians. Indonesians do not socialize exclusively within their own ethnic group.

The main groups are the Javanese (40.6 percent), followed by the Sundanese (15 percent), Madurese (3.3 percent), and Minangkabau

(2.7 percent). Java was the home of Indonesia's older civilizations and the center of the Dutch administration in the colonial days, so the Javanese have had the most contact with the outside world. They have developed a more cosmopolitan culture as a consequence. Among other groups, such as the Dayaks in Kalimantan and the Irianese who live in remote areas, some may never have seen a foreigner.

ACEHNESE The Caucasian-looking Acehnese of northwest Sumatra are staunch Muslims. They are fine craftsmen and boat builders. Aceh, in north Sumatra, was a major trading center for centuries and the first point where Islam arrived in Indonesia.

BADUI The Badui are a tiny ethnic group of 5,000—8,000 centered in the isolated Kendeng Mountains of West Java where they first fled to escape the spread of Islam. Here they live by strict beliefs that are all their own, and they are forbidden to take any form of transportation or learn writing, which is believed to have "secret powers." The white-robed "inner" Badui who live in the heart of the homeland are even stricter and are believed to have mystic and clairvoyant powers.

DAYAKS The isolated Dayaks, who have a rich tradition of art, live in longhouses along rivers in the jungles of Kalimantan. They use blowpipes for hunting. Although many have converted to Christianity, they retain some animists beliefs—they believe that spirits dwell in many things, especially the life-providing river. Headhunting died out many decades ago. The practices of tattooing and wearing several metal earrings to elongate the ear lobes are regarded as beautiful.

BALINESE The Balinese are Hindu and their religion determines much of their lifestyle. The preparations for elaborate temple, cremation, and other ceremonies take up much of their energies. Balinese art is world famous, with each village specializing in a particular creative craft.

A Toranjan woman dressed in traditional clothing.

BATAK The sturdy Bataks live in north-central Sumatra. Many Bataks are Christians, with the largest Batak Christian group living around the picturesque Lake Toba. They are a proud, conservative people. Many are musically inclined and become singers and band leaders.

JAVANESE The Javanese make up more than half of Indonesia's population. Java has always been the center of Indonesian history because its rich volcanic soils have supported a large population. This explains its highly developed culture, art, and language. Today rural Javanese live in overcrowded villages and grow rice on tiny plots.

MINANGKABAU Traditionally the Minangkabau are a matrilineal society where the women are the inheritors of the family's wealth and where the man lives with the woman's family after marriage. Divorce and remarriage are common, as is migration outside the people's native region of West Sumatra. There has always been a large Minangkabau representation in politics and government.

MINAHASA The Minahasa are Christians and largely Eurasian—that is, of European and Asian descent. Because their homeland, northern Sulawesi, is close to the Philippines, there are cultural links between the two. The Minahasa are well known for their lavish feasts and large gatherings.

BUGIS Ever since the 14th century the Bugis have been the dreaded sea pirates of the Indonesian waters in their colorful, wind-driven sailboats. They are expert boat makers and have been traders for centuries. They sail without compasses, claiming that they can "smell" tidal waves or approaching coral reefs.

SUNDANESE The Sundanese occupy the western third of Java. They are famous for their *wayang golek* (wooden puppets) and the haunting sounds of their hollow flutes.

TORAJANESE The Torajanese are rugged, mountain-dwelling people famous for the eerie effigies of their dead that guard limestone cliffs in central Sulawesi. Although today most Torajanese are Christians, they still practice some traditional forms of worship involving wearing headdresses of buffalo horns, sacrificing the animal on important occasions, and giving buffaloes to the bride's family in marriages.

CHINESE Chinese traders have been coming to Indonesia since the time of the Sriwajaya Empire (7th to 12th century), and established coastal communities from the 1500s. In the late 19th century large numbers of Chinese men came to Indonesia to work on Dutch plantations and in mines. Chinese womenfolk were only allowed to emigrate to Indonesia from the early 20th century, to join their menfolk. Today many members of this large ethnic group have intermarried and taken local names. Totok Chinese are first-generation Chinese in Indonesia.

INTERNET LINKS

http://travel.nationalgeographic.com/travel/countries/indonesia-photos/
This site has a diverse collection of evocative photographs showing many aspects of Indonesia and Indonesian life.

www.lonelyplanet.com/indonesia/bali/images
This site provides an outstanding collection of photographs showing life on the island of Bali.

LIFESTYLE

Motorcyclists and their passengers stop for a quick chat on a seemingly precarious boardwalk between two sections of the village.

NDONESIAN LIFESTYLE is determined by *adat* (AAH-dut) or custom. This is an unwritten code of traditional behavior that is found in every city, town, village, and farm. It is not a part of religion, but it contains rules of conduct for almost every situation.

There are many *adat* or customs for different ethnic groups in Indonesia. Besides covering behavior and taboos, they also govern matters such as ownership of land, inheritance rights, marriage and

Young people getting around by means of a sampan, or small boat.

7

Lifestyle in Indonesia depends very much on income, as it does in many countries. However, all Indonesians, whether rich or poor, believe in the importance of family and community.

death ceremonies, the type of food that may be eaten, and the general way of life. All Indonesians practice some form of *adat*, although practices differ among groups. With information freely available through the Internet, television, and movies, Western influence in music, fashion, movies, and junk food are diluting the importance of *adat*, especially in the cities, where academic achievement and economic power are emphasized. However, *adat* still has an influence on an Indonesian's core customs and behaviors.

THE SOCIAL WEB

It is extremely important in Indonesia to conform to the group rather than be different. "Doing your own thing," or deviating from the accepted behavior, is considered embarrassing and unnatural.

The first allegiance is to the family. In Indonesia, however, the family extends to grandparents, uncles, aunts, first cousins, and even second cousins. In the big cities anyone from the same village is called *saudara* (sah-hu-DAH-

A family enjoying a day out together. Indonesians value their families, including extended ones, very highly.

rah), or relative. The family provides emotional and financial support, and relatives can be relied upon to help out in many situations—from paying for a child's education or a grandparent's medical bill to providing emotional support in times of crisis.

After the family Indonesians have loyalties to their clan (rarely), village, mosque, neighborhood, and work-related organizations.

BEING A GOOD JAVANESE

Many aspects of Javanese culture have become associated with Indonesia because the Javanese are the country's largest ethnic group. Javanese culture has been influenced by Hindu culture, which has refined social behavior. Visitors are quickly struck by the intricate rules of etiquette and the concern with politeness.

The Javanese do not like anything startling or unpredictable to disturb their single, seamless vision of the world. When something unpleasant

A group of young Javanese children enjoying a ride.

cannot be avoided, however, it is dealt with by maintaining an outward calm. Many foreigners are startled when the tragic news of a dying child or loss of property is told with a smile, or even a nervous laugh. No Javanese thinks it funny; a smile just masks their feelings.

Indonesians hate confrontation, preferring to hide negative feelings such as jealousy and anger. They do not complain or shout, but cope with stress by smiling and quietly withdrawing. If pushed beyond limits, however, an Indonesian can lose control or even run amok in blind anger; in fact the word *amok* originated in this region.

Even in conversation a Javanese ideally strives to "maintain the peace." This often means speaking in a roundabout, indirect manner—to ask for a glass of water, a person might clear his throat and comment on how dry and dusty the day is.

The Javanese way of life is also seen in their elaborate rules of etiquette. It is very important to show correct form and politeness, especially to elders. People talk in low, calm tones with no dramatic arm gestures, even in times of great excitement. To Javanese extreme emotions such as uncontrollable laughter or wails of sorrow indicate a lack of self-control and refinement.

UNIQUE CHARACTERISTICS

FLEXIBLE TIME Indonesians treat time in their own way. The day begins at sunset, so "last night" is considered earlier the same day. In many social situations Indonesians have a laidback approach to punctuality—a person can arrive an hour to three hours late without causing offense. When you ask someone the time it is rounded off to the nearest quarter or even half hour; there is no need to be precise.

BATHING Indonesians bathe at least twice a day and the more water that gets splashed around, the cleaner and better. In a typical bathroom one does not climb into the stone water storage basin or *mandi* (MAHN-dee). Tepid water is splashed from this *mandi* over oneself for an invigorating bath, which leaves everything soaking wet.

Most rural homes do not have toilets, and people simply use a nearby stream. A squat toilet is usually a hole in the ground with footrests on either side. There is usually no flush system or toilet paper, as water is preferred for reasons of hygiene.

SICKNESS Most Indonesians prefer to have mild illnesses treated at home. They believe that sickness can be caused by *masuk angin* (mah-SOOK AHNG-in), literally "the entrance of wind." To protect against this Indonesians wrap themselves in warm clothes. It is common to see workers wearing zipped-up black leather jackets under the intense midday sun.

To alleviate many common ailments that are caused by *masuk angin*, oil is rubbed onto a person's neck and back with a heavy metal coin that is vigorously scraped along the skin. The deep red stripes that remain for a day or two actually look much worse than they feel.

INTIMACY Public displays of intimacy between people of the opposite sex are considered improper, although it is perfectly acceptable for friends of the same sex to walk hand in hand. Kissing in public is taboo.

FORGIVENESS Asking forgiveness for any errors made is a part of the national ethic and the main feature of Javanese politeness. At Lebaran, the end of the fasting month, Muslims formally beg forgiveness for wrongdoings of the past year from family and friends. When leaving a job the same is done of one's colleagues and superiors. The apology is always accepted gracefully so that everyone feels purified.

A young boy from Aceh takes a quick shower from a communal tap in Paloh village.

SEMANGAT, THE LIFE FORCE

Many things in nature are believed to contain a vital energy or life force called semangat (ser-mahng-aht).

Some believe that in a person semangat *is contained in the head, blood, heart, hair, and nails. Children are not patted on the head, which is considered sacred, and clippings of nails and hair are carefully disposed of, because these can be used for sorcery. A child's first haircut is a significant event, and tying together a few strands of the bride's and groom's hair symbolizes the strength of their union. Dayak headhunters believed that returning home with enemy heads augmented one's powers, just as the power of a* keris *(KER-is) (dagger) increased with the number of times it had drawn blood.*

There are ritual precautions to appease the spirits contained in important crops such as rice. Clothes, sacred heirlooms, and jewelry are believed to contain the soul of the previous owner. The semangat *of mountains, lakes, and old trees must also be handled with respect.*

THE *SELAMATAN*

All Indonesians have in common the *selamatan* (ser-lah-maht-ahn). This communal thanksgiving feast celebrates turning points in an individual's life, such as birth, circumcision, marriage, death, and the start or completion of a major project. It is also an indicator of a person's wealth and status, usually measured by the numbers in attendance. Every effort is made to ensure that this number is large. However, the feast can vary depending on the ethnic group, status, age (the young prefer to simplify things), and the wealth of the family.

The host provides the entertainment: a *gamelan* or *wayang* performance. Nowadays taped music played on loudspeakers is also popular and creates a festive mood. Special ceremonial foods are prepared, incense is burned, and Islamic prayers are intoned. In the royal courts even larger *selamatans* are held on religious occasions.

PREGNANCY AND BIRTH: TRADITIONAL PRACTICES

The seventh month of a pregnancy is celebrated on most islands with a ritual bath for the mother-to-be. On Java there is a ceremony where the pregnant woman prepares a special spicy fruit salad and "sells" it to guests who pay for it with roof tiles. It is believed the sale teaches frugality to the child, and the taste of the salad indicates the baby's sex—sour for a boy and sweet for a girl.

Throughout her pregnancy the mother is given specially prepared food and is not allowed to touch sharp objects such as knives and scissors, which might harm the child. No gifts are given for an unborn child because overzealous actions and words are believed to invite evil.

Once the child is born it is guarded through its first five years. Every ethnic group has a different welcoming ceremony for the baby. In Java the destiny of the child is predicted by placing various objects such as a book, pen, and some gold in front of the child to see which object attracts its attention first. Special threads with amulets put around the child's arms or neck protect it against evil, and daily doses of special infant *jamu* (JAH-moo), or herbal medicine, keep the child safe. In the towns and cities, modern health-care practices are also common.

THE GROWING-UP YEARS

Children are particularly treasured in Indonesia. Babies are always kept slung comfortably and securely at the mother's hip in a long, narrow piece of batik, called a *selendang* (SER-land-dang).

A child can demand to be carried this way for several years, or at least until the arrival of the next child. In this *selendang* the child can be fed on demand rather than at set times.

Everyone in Indonesia has a certain status and knows his or her proper place. There is security in this knowledge, and nobody wants to disturb the peace by upsetting the hierarchy. Children soon learn that, within the family,

A boy wears a traditional hat during festivities at a Muslim circumcision festival in Lombok.

status is arranged in a hierarchical order according to age rather than sex, with the father being right at the top. As in many societies mothers have a greater role in bringing up children.

In the workplace this carries over to the "whatever pleases the boss" philosophy of many Indonesians. *Bapak* (BAA-pak) is the word for "father," but it is also used for anyone who is senior in age or status. No effort is spared to please anyone occupying the father-figure position. The boss is told what he wants to hear, true feelings and facts are covered up, and arguing with superiors is considered rude. Direct eye contact may be misinterpreted as a challenge, so the Javanese speak to superiors with downcast eyes in as humble a stance as possible.

Often children are raised by the wider community and become very attached to an older relative—sometimes more so than their own parents. The grandparents often take full responsibility, financial and otherwise, for one grandchild. Children in turn help out with household chores, although a grandson is pampered more than a granddaughter and is only expected to run the occasional errand.

Children are only considered grown-up once they get married. Until then they live with their parents, help out financially with the household expenses, and fulfill the social obligations expected of them. Once they are married the bride either lives in her husband's home, or the couple gets a place of their own. The exception is found in the Minangkabau matrilineal system in West Sumatra where the reverse occurs—the groom joins the bride's family. Titles, wealth, and family names are all passed down the female line. Men look after family heirlooms, but it is the women who hold the keys.

When Muslim boys reach the age of 11, they undergo circumcision to mark their passage into manhood.

In the past they would anaesthetize themselves with icy cold water before the event. Today there are mass circumcisions using modern medical equipment in most villages.

Sometimes the boys are dressed up as princes and paraded through town on ponies or decorated becaks. A selamatan *usually follows the circumcision ceremony.*

Most Indonesian families are very close-knit and keep in contact, even when they are separated by a great distance. The annual family reunion takes place at Lebaran when everyone comes together to celebrate and exchange news.

MARRIAGE

In Indonesia everyone is expected to marry. In the rural areas most Indonesians marry at a young age; in the cities marriage takes place later. By the time a rural girl reaches the age of 19, she is probably not only married but also a mother.

Indonesians believe that eventually everyone will get married. Even a 60-year-old bachelor replies to the question, "Are you married?" with a standard *belum* (BEH-loom), meaning "not yet." Muslim law permits a man to have up to four wives, but this is less common in modern Indonesia.

Wedding ceremonies are among the most elaborate and colorful occasions in Indonesia. The most ornate ethnic costumes are worn and lavish gifts, including gold, money, fruit, and flowers, are exchanged. The bride and groom sit in regal style on ornate thrones placed on a raised platform and do not mix with guests except to say thank you when the guests file past to congratulate them. The number of guests invited to a wedding can range from a few hundred to more than a thousand. Some families spend so much on wedding feasts that they end up in debt.

Indonesian traditional wedding clothes are detailed and intricate.

In Balinese weddings it is traditional for the bride to be ceremonially "kidnapped" by the bridegroom. The honeymoon precedes the actual wedding, which occurs about a month after the "abduction."

DEATH AND FUNERALS

Funeral ceremonies vary with the religion and customs of different people. A Muslim is buried within 24 hours of death and colleagues, friends, and relatives arrive within hours to pay their respects to the deceased, regardless of how close they were. There is no weeping, as this is considered an indication of a weak soul and an invitation to spirits.

It is believed that when a person dies his spirit must be properly "managed" or it will cause havoc in the world of the living. To prevent the soul from returning to Earth, some rites are designed to confuse it. In Sumatra the body is sent out of the house through a small gap in the floor, which is then sealed. In Bali and Sulawesi the hearse is jolted and jarred to prevent the spirit from finding its way back. For the soul to successfully make it to the land of the ancestors—usually in the form of a bird or insect—proper funeral rites are essential. Although these vary by region and ethnic group, they are often colorful and extravagant spectacles.

If a family cannot afford this expense at the time of death, the body is either kept wrapped in shrouds in the house or temporarily buried until enough money is saved for the rites. In Bali the bereaved wait for more deaths so they can have a joint cremation. The bones are then exhumed, cleaned, and given a proper send-off.

The dead are never forgotten in Indonesia: Among the Torajanese, eerie effigies of the dead line the cliff faces, their final burial place; in Irian Jaya, the skull and bones of the deceased are preserved; and all over Indonesia graves or symbolic statues are carefully tended as they contain the benevolent spirits of ancestors. In keeping with their Hindu religion, the Balinese cremate their dead.

INTERNET LINKS

www.orientalarchitecture.com/indonesia/laketoba/bataktobahouses.php
This site describes the Batak people of Sumatra, with photographs of their unique homes.

www.weddinginspirasi.com/2010/01/06/angel-paris-indonesian-wedding-dress-kebaya
This website provides an example of some very beautiful Indonesian wedding dresses.

www.panoramas.dk/fullscreen6/f28-bali-funeral.html
This site shows a Balinese funeral, with a funeral pyre, through a panoramic, 360-degree view.

RELIGION

The Baiturrahman Mosque in Banda Aceh.

FOUR OF THE MAJOR RELIGIONS OF the world are officially recognized in Indonesia—Hinduism, Buddhism, Islam, and Christianity. In the spirit of Pancasila (or Five Principles), there is freedom of religion.

In 2009, 86.1 percent of Indonesians were Muslims, 5.7 percent Protestants, 3 percent Roman Catholics, 2 percent Hindus, 1 percent Buddhists, with the remainder adhering to other beliefs or none at all. These religions were introduced from overseas—Hinduism and Buddhism from India, Islam by Muslim traders from India and the Middle East, and Christianity by the Europeans.

ASSIMILATION OF DIFFERENT BELIEFS

These different religions were absorbed into Indonesia, and yet they did not erase the original animistic beliefs and traditional customs (*adat*) that had existed for centuries. These religions were layered one on top of the other, each layer interacting with but never quite replacing the one before it. The earliest system of belief was animism, or belief in spirits (often of ancestors) contained within natural objects, such as mountains, trees, rice, rain, and the sun.

Hinduism and Buddhism came later and intermingled with animism. Then, when Islam and Christianity arrived centuries later, these too were modified and adapted to fit with the existing mixture of *adat*, animism, and Hindu-Buddhist beliefs.

8

Islam is the religion of the majority of Indonesians. However, the country is tolerant of all the world's major religions, and large numbers of Indonesians practice Hinduism, Christianity, and Buddhism.

Muslim girls reciting verses from the Koran.

Indonesia is the world's largest Islamic nation (with about 202 million Muslims). The Javanese and the Minangkabau of Sumatra make up the largest group of Muslims. Hinduism is mainly found on the island of Bali, while Christianity is found in pockets throughout the archipelago, such as in Sumatra, Kalimantan, Nusa Tenggara, and northern Sulawesi. Most Chinese are Buddhists, Confucianists, and Christians.

In the Moluccas (or Maluku) Islands, which were at the center of the Dutch spice trade, small Christian communities originally converted by the Dutch can still be found. Flores has a Catholic population that was converted by Portuguese missionaries. In other areas animist beliefs and practices predominate, especially in Kalimantan and Irian Jaya.

ISLAM

Islam was first brought to Indonesia by Indian merchants, and later by Arab traders around the eighth century A.D. It was first established in Aceh in northern Sumatra, from which it later spread throughout the Indonesian archipelago. Today the Muslim population is concentrated in Java and Sumatra, which are also the most populous areas of Indonesia. In other areas the Muslim population is more scattered.

An Indonesian proverb says: "Religion comes in from the sea, but customs come down from the mountains."

Islam preached the equality and brotherhood of man, an idea that appealed to people who were tired of being at the bottom of the rigid and hierarchical Hindu caste system. The few communities that resisted conversion, such as the Badui and the Torajanese, fled to the interior as Islam spread through the coastal areas.

THE CALL TO PRAYER

Muslims traditionally pray five times a day: at sunset, night, dawn, noon, and afternoon. The prayer times are published in the papers, broadcast over radio and television, and sounded in mosques all over the country.

Every Friday Muslim men go to the nearest mosque for prayers, while women pray at home. A strict ritual must be followed before prayers begin.

First the faithful must purify their bodies by washing. The hands are washed, and then the mouth is cleansed by gargling and spitting. The face is then washed, followed by the lower arms up to the elbows. Then the head is moistened and the hair is combed with water. Finally both feet are washed up to the ankles. All this is repeated three times in strict order and always starting with the right side.

Special clothes for prayers are also required. Women wrap themselves in a white gown from head to toe, while the men wrap a sarong around their waist.

In the mosque there are also rules to follow. Shoes should be left outside. Muslims are also careful not to touch any unclean objects before and during prayer. Muslims greet fellow worshipers with the words as-salaam alaikum *(ehs seh-LAHM eh-lei-koom), meaning "peace to you," and respond with* wa alaikum salaam *(weh eh-LEI-koom seh-LAHM), meaning "and upon you, peace." Then the prayers begin with the* muezzin's *(moo-EZ-in) call to prayer, which begins with* Allahu akbar *(ehl-LAH ho-EHK-behr), meaning "God is great."*

Islam is a way of life, a practical rather than merely theoretical religion. Today it pervades every aspect of Indonesian life: Mosques with loudspeakers call the faithful to prayer five times a day; Friday, the Islamic holy day, is a half-working day; pigs are not very often found because they are seen as unclean; most public places have a little room set aside for prayer; public toilets are equipped with running water for washing; men are allowed to take up to four wives at a time; and many Indonesians save money to make the hajj or holy journey to Mecca.

Indonesia has a dual education system, with both a general school system and a religious educational system. Islam is studied for a certain number of hours each week at all levels in the general school system.

The Islam practiced by individual communities' ranges from the ultra-orthodox to nominal Muslims. The people of central Java practice an Islam mingled with animism and Hindu-Javanese mysticism. For instance, when a person is ill, the *dukun* (DOO-koon) or folk doctor writes Islamic prayers on pieces of paper and dunks them in a glass of water for the patient to drink. Once the water has been drunk, the prayers supposedly fight the demon that is causing the illness.

Extreme religious conservatism is rare in Indonesia. Although the Acehnese are known to be strict Muslims, most Indonesian Muslims have a more liberal attitude toward religion. Women, for instance, are much freer than their sisters in other Islamic countries. They do not necessarily wear facial veils but instead wear very colorful blouses (called *bajus*) with figure-hugging sarong skirts instead. Wearing headscarves has become more common over the years. A husband has to get permission from his first wife before taking a second wife, and women are allowed to initiate divorce.

Hindu pilgrims with sacrificial offerings arrive at Agung volcano.

HINDUISM

Hinduism arrived in Indonesia from India more than 1,500 years ago. Of all the religions that were transplanted in Indonesia, it made the greatest impact. Even the coming of Islam did not destroy all remaining Hindu culture.

Many traces of Hinduism's great past and influence still linger today, especially in Java and Bali. The palaces of Solo (Surabaya) and Yogyakarta are still cultural reminders of this long-gone period; the characters and stories of Javanese classical dance and puppetry are based on the ancient

Balinese Hinduism is a unique combination of animist and Hindu beliefs. Hindu beliefs are seen in the Balinese belief in the Trinity of Gods—Brahma the Creator, Vishnu the Preserver, and Shiva the Destroyer—and the all-important cremation of the dead to release the spirit, enabling it to participate in the cycle of reincarnation. The Balinese knowledge of the Hindu epics forms the basis of many of their dance and other art forms.

The Balinese also practice ancestor worship, blood sacrifices, and mysticism. They often go into trances and are possessed by the gods and demons surrounding them in nature. They have numerous rites and sacrifices—hardly a day goes by without a ceremony aimed at keeping peace with the forces of nature. In fact, these endless colorful and elaborate temple ceremonies are a major tourist attraction.

Hindu epics the Mahabharata and Ramayana; numerous Hindu ruins and ancient monuments, such as Prambanan, are scattered all over the island; the Garuda, the mount of Lord Vishnu the Preserver, is Indonesia's national emblem; and Sanskrit, the language of Hinduism, is found in Javanese and Indonesian words, place names, and even the state motto, Pancasila.

Today Indonesia's Hindu population is found on the islands of Bali. Many of its people are the descendants of the Majapahits who fled from Java to escape Muslim invaders. The rich Hindu-Javanese culture, religion, and philosophy they brought with them were combined with existing Balinese animism, giving rise to today's unique Balinese Hinduism.

BUDDHISM

Hinduism and Buddhism have coexisted on Java for over a thousand years. Both originated in India, with Hinduism being based on the religion of the original Aryan settlers, as expounded in texts such as the Vedas, Bhagavad Gita, and Upanishads. Buddhists believe that life is full of suffering caused by desire, and that the way to halt this endless cycle of birth and death is through Enlightenment.

The Chinese and Tenggerese account for the major Buddhist sects. Other smaller Buddhist groups are also found in Java around the cities of Solo (Surakarta), Yogyakarta, and Cirebon.

CHRISTIANITY

Despite being under European colonial rule for centuries, only 8 percent of Indonesia's population is Christian. The Christian population is scattered and found in pockets in certain parts of western Sumatra, the islands of Flores and Timor, northern Sulawesi, Maluku, and in parts of Kalimantan.

Buddhist monks stand before the statue of the Buddha at Borobudur on Waisak Day (the Buddha's birthday).

The Christianity practiced by most ethnic groups, whether Protestant or Catholic, has intermingled with local beliefs, producing some interesting customs such as the barefoot Easter procession in the dead of night in Flores, gamelan-led masses in Yogyakarta, and bull-sacrifices among the Torajanese Christians in Sulawesi.

ANIMISM

Animism is a belief in the world of spirits, and the belief that objects can have inner powers. These beliefs are found all over Indonesia where people's religious faith is influenced by spirits in such objects as rice, trees, rivers, rocks, the sun, and rain. Many people also believe that the spirits of dead ancestors live on.

Animist beliefs are mainly practiced by Indonesia's hill communities and other isolated social groups, especially in Kalimantan, Papua, and West Papua. However, even the Muslims, Hindus, Buddhists, and Christians of Indonesia retain some animist beliefs.

GHOSTS AND GENIES In Java, when children do not sleep, they are told of the dreadful *way-way* (way-way), the frightener of small children. In Sulawesi it is the *pok-pok* (poke-poke), the flying head, while in Bali, they fear the *leyaks* (leh-YAHKS) who kidnap troublesome children.

Stories of ghosts, goddesses, demons, spirits, and genies abound. Buffalo heads are placed in the foundations of new buildings to appease the spirits, with priests often flying sacrificial heads to offshore oil rigs by helicopter for the same purpose. Witch doctors exorcise evil from temples, swimming pools, cars, and hotels. Any transition in life—birth, circumcision, marriage, death—is accompanied by rituals and elaborate meals in the traditional *selamatan* ceremony.

And every Indonesian fears the queen of the South Seas, the spiritual wife of the sultan of Yogyakarta, who seizes anyone wearing a green swimsuit to become a soldier in her army. Most hotels along the south coast of Java conform to superstition by keeping one room locked and specially reserved for when the queen visits!

INTERNET LINKS

www.islamicpopulation.com/asia/Indonesia/Islam%20in%20Indonesia.html

This website offers a detailed history and analysis of Islam in Indonesia, with maps, statistics, and photographs.

www.nytimes.com/slideshow/2008/01/28/world/20080128MYSTICISM_index.html

This site shows a series of images with captions explaining Javanese mystical beliefs in relation to the Javanese landscape.

www.buddhanet.net/e-learning/buddhistworld/indo-txt.htm

This site offers a brief account of Buddhism in Indonesia with statistics and photographs.

LANGUAGE

Newspapers at a newsstand in Indonesia.

LOOKING AT INDIVIDUAL ISLANDS, one may think that people in Java speak Javanese, people in Bali speak Balinese, and the Madura people speak Madurese. This is not the case as different regions and ethnic groups within each island have different local dialects.

On Java, for example, Javanese, Sundanese, and Madurese are all spoken, and there are 15 major languages on Sumatra. Other languages spoken in Indonesia include Acehnese, Batak, Sasak, Tetum, Dayak, Minahasa, Toraja, Buginese, Halmahera, Ambonese, Ceramese, and several Irianese languages. Many of these languages are also spoken in different dialects, which make for a more colorful culture and society. For instance Sulawesi alone has 62 documented languages and countless more dialects.

ONE PEOPLE, ONE LANGUAGE, ONE NATION

With such linguistic variety it is easy to see why the Indonesian motto, *Bhinneka Tunggal Ika* (BHEE-nay-kah TOONG-gahl EE-kah), meaning "unity in diversity," is of such significance. Since

Right: Newspapers for sale.

the number of languages in use could cause problems of communication, in 1928, Bahasa Indonesia (literally meaning "the language of Indonesia") was chosen as a unifying language to bridge the cultural and linguistic gap across all of Indonesia's scattered islands. Indonesian is used in all official communications and throughout the media and in business. Although every Indonesian learns to speak Indonesian fluently, most also speak their local or ethnic dialect on an everyday basis, too. It is very common to hear people mixing and matching languages, depending on the circumstances. They might begin a sentence in Indonesian, but interject the odd phrase from their local dialect if they think it makes the meaning clearer.

Javanese is the second most widely used language in Indonesia after Bahasa Indonesia, spoken by 84 million people. This is because the majority of the Indonesian population lives on Java, and because Java is still the center of much of Indonesia's industry and commerce. Dutch is still spoken by some of the older generation, but English is the most popular foreign language taught in schools. Even so, few people speak English well.

A *becak* rider reads the newspaper while waiting for passengers.

Students helping each other with a school assignment.

BAHASA INDONESIA

Bahasa Indonesia, the national language, is derived from Malay, which has been the language of trade throughout Southeast Asia for centuries. The language is derived from the Malay dialect written in the Riau islands, between Sumatra and Singapore. It is written in the Roman script and is one of the simplest languages in the world. It has no tenses, grammatical gender, or tones. It is easy to learn the language for simple communication, but more difficult to master the refined variety with its strict grammatical rules. It is a democratic language without the language levels that are present in Javanese, Sundanese, and Balinese. Indonesian is also a culturally neutral language and is not attached to any particular ethnic group, despite its origins in the Riau archipelago.

It was introduced as the national language of Indonesia in 1928 when Indonesian nationalist leaders realized that freedom from Dutch colonial

JAVANESE—THE LANGUAGE OF HIERARCHY

Imagine a language so complex that the words to say can be expressed in five ways: kandha, sanjang, criyos, matur, or ngendika. The word used depends on the "level" of speech chosen. And the level depends on the person speaking, to whom the words are addressed, their relative ages and status, the situation, sex, generation, the race of the speaker, and so on.

Javanese speech is divided into three levels: Ngoko, Madya, and Krama. Each has different words for everyday things. Ngoko is the first language a child learns and is simple, unrefined, and used between close friends. The highest level is Krama, an elegant and polite speech used in formal situations. In between these is Madya speech, used when people of low status talk or when two close friends speak respectfully. In addition there is low Krama and high Krama to indicate the status of the speakers, and other levels of speech used only for royalty and ritual feasts.

This complex, hierarchical language has been heavily influenced by the Indian caste system, where everyone must be addressed according to their rank. To use the wrong word would be insulting, and to speak on the wrong level can be socially disastrous. No wonder the Javanese find it easier to speak in Bahasa Indonesia!

rule also meant that they had to find a truly national Indonesian language. Previously the nationalist leaders had communicated in Dutch. In the famous "Youth Pledge" of 1928, three ideals were adopted: One Fatherland, Indonesia; One Nation, Indonesia; and, One Language, Bahasa Indonesia—the language of unity.

When the Japanese invaded in the 1940s they also encouraged Bahasa Indonesia to be spoken as a language that would foster Indonesian nationalism and encourage local resistance to the old colonial powers. Their efforts were very successful. Bahasa Indonesia became so widespread that after independence there was no question of changing the national language.

The long history of contact between Indonesia and the rest of the world can be seen in the large number of Bahasa Indonesia words that have been borrowed from other languages. There are more than 7,000 Dutch words (for

A group of taxi drivers taking a break and having a chat.

example, *meubel* for "furniture"); Portuguese words (for instance the island of Flores is named after the Portuguese word for "flowers"); English words (*doktor* and *bis* for "doctor" and "bus"); and numerous Sanskrit, Arabic, Polynesian, Tagalog, Chinese, French, and Spanish words.

BODY LANGUAGE

Indonesians are very reserved in their body movements and gestures. Unnecessarily flinging arms, jerking the head, and talking loudly (even in anger) is considered *kasar* (KAH-sar), or unrefined. Sometimes the implications of facial expressions, gestures, and other body signals say as much as, if not more than, the message in the words alone.

Here are some examples of body language peculiar to Indonesians:

THE HEAD AND THE FEET The head and the feet are, by virtue of their position, the most and least esteemed parts of the body, respectively. The head contains the "life force" and is thus considered sacred. In the past headhunters (such as the Dayaks of Kalimantan and Torajanese of Sulawesi) would bring back enemy heads for good luck. Children should never be patted on the head. Respect is also shown by keeping one's head lower than the other person's.

Care must be taken with one's feet: Pointing them at someone is disrespectful, and propping them up on a table is absolutely taboo.

GREETING   In greetings there is no effusive hugging and kissing, just a respectful Islamic handshake. This is done by holding both the hands of the other person, then letting go and bringing your hands back to the chest. In social circles, however, the ladies kiss each other on both cheeks in the Dutch-style.

STANDING   In most situations Indonesians stand with a humble and respectful posture: the hands lightly overlapped in front of the body and the head slightly bowed. When speaking to someone of higher status, Indonesians lower their eyes to show respect. Standing with the hands on the hips is aggressive, and holding them behind the back is considered too superior.

Friendly children smile for the camera.

WALKING   When in a restricted space, one should ask permission before walking in front of someone. This is done by bending low, extending the right arm forward, mumbling a *permisi* (per-MEE-see), meaning "please give me permission," or "excuse me," and then quickly walking across.

POINTING Indonesians only point with their thumb. Using any other finger is considered rude. The gesture is like a gentler version of that used in America for hitching a ride, but with a more open palm. This gesture is also used like a "go ahead" signal when asking someone to proceed. For instance it is used to invite someone to begin eating by pointing at the food.

GESTURES   Rude or obscene signs are seldom seen. One different gesture is the one indicating insanity. Instead of circling the index finger at the ear, the hand is used in a sawing motion across the forehead.

SMILING   Everyone smiles in Indonesia, but it does not always indicate happiness. The Javanese are known to giggle when they are sad, smile when they give bad news, and laugh when they are nervous or confused. This does not show amusement, but indicates their belief that life should remain as calm and unruffled as possible.

INTERNET LINKS

www.omniglot.com/language/phrases/indonesian.php

This website offers a list of the most useful Indonesian phrases, with their English translations.

www.omniglot.com/writing/javanese.htm

This site describes the history and development of the Javanese language, with a list of all the letters of the Javanese alphabet and their translation in the English alphabet.

The beautiful detail of a batik cloth design.

10

INDONESIA HAS A GREAT VARIETY OF folk and classical arts, all of which are an integral part of traditional life. Its shadow puppets and printed textiles are world-famous. Indonesian arts have been influenced by foreign cultures, especially ancient Indian and Chinese civilizations.

Two main art traditions are old Malay, which is the tradition in the remote interiors of Sumatra and Borneo; and the Javanese and Balinese styles, which are influenced by the Hindu stories of the *Mahabharata* and

A statue depicting the *Ramayana* story near the Ngurah Rai Airport.

Ramayana. Bali is of special cultural interest because its art traditions have remained untouched by the influence of Islam. Its art is heavily influenced by Hindu-Buddhist temple art, seen in the vegetal offerings and the beautifully stylized and symbolic palm leaf objects.

The most sophisticated dance and art forms are found in Java, and for many centuries, were limited to the courts. The practice of gamelan music, *wayang* drama, and the age-old batik-making used to be strictly royal traditions. In the distant past these arts were practiced only by ladies of the nobility or by specially commissioned artists. The royal monopoly on classical dance, for instance, was not broken until 1918 when the first school was set up outside the palace walls.

MUSIC

Performed to accompany dance and drama, gamelan music is Indonesia's most important and historical musical art form; its roots can be traced

A traditional gamelan orchestra performing.

"Everybody in Bali seems to be an artist. Coolies (an unskilled laborer) and princes, priests and peasants, men and women alike, can dance, play musical instruments, paint, or carve in wood and stone. It was often surprising to discover that an otherwise poor and dilapidated village harbored an elaborate temple, a great orchestra, or a group of actors of repute."
—Miguel Covarrubias, *Island of Bali* (1937)

The angklung *is a simple portable instrument made from hollow bamboo tubes of various lengths suspended in a frame.*

When the angklung *frame is shaken, it produces a musical tinkling sound that is similar to the sound of the xylophone. In the olden days it was used to accompany armies that were marching into battle. It is especially popular in western Java today, although it is now used in gamelan orchestras and is played in school bands.*

back over 1,500 years. Gamelan music sounds marvelously fluid, something between jazz and the gentle rippling of water. Traditionally gamelan music was not notated and was taught orally; however, in the 19th century, the kratons of Yogyakarta and Surakarta developed distinct notations for transcribing the popular repertoire.

Today gamelan accompanies dance, theater, and royal and religious festivities; it is even performed in mosques, but in keeping with Javanese *adat*.

There are two distinct versions of gamelan: the slow, stately, measured Javanese gamelan and the Balinese version that explodes with energy and vibrancy. A full gamelan orchestra has a combination of xylophones, drums, gongs, string instruments, and flutes. Depending on how important the occasion is, an orchestra may have between five and 80 instruments and musicians. Unlike most Western music, gamelan has a unique two-scale tuning method. This means every set has a distinctive sound based on the preference of the maker.

Drums are usually the most important instrument in a gamelan orchestra, because they set the tempo. However, there can be regional differences in the musical instruments used: In western Java, the *angklung* (AHNG-klong) is important, while in eastern Java a zither or string instrument is more popular. Central Java gamelan has a more elaborate form than western Java, and Balinese gamelan is the liveliest of all.

"There is something so extremely simple, and at the same time gay, in the sound produced by the rattling of these bamboo tubes, that I confess I have never heard the *angklung* without pleasure."
—Sir Stamford Raffles, in *A History of Java*

Dancers perform a dance, telling the story of *Ramayana*.

DANCE

Indonesia's dance tradition is closely associated with rituals such as exorcising spirits; performing rite of passage ceremonies, such as birth, circumcision, and death; and celebrating the agricultural calendar. Besides entertainment these dances also serve as important religious and cultural rituals.

Traditional and folk dances are vibrant, energetic, and require little formal training, but the famous classical dances of Java and Bali are quite the opposite. These dance traditions are heavily influenced by Indian cultural dance styles, as seen in the dance postures: bent knees, turned-out legs, straight body with head tilted to one side, and use of hand gestures.

Javanese classical dance is calm, controlled, and subtle. The dancer's eyes are always downcast, the limbs kept close to the body, and there are long, silent, hypnotizing pauses. On the other hand Balinese dance is energetic. The dancers burst onto the stage, often to the sound of gongs and cymbals, with eyes wide open and arms held high, often darting around in a manner that is totally different from the more refined Javanese version of classical dance.

The two main schools of Javanese dance are in Yogyakarta and Solo. Training starts when a child is six years old. It often takes years to perfect just one gesture, such as the arching of the fingers backward to touch the forearm.

More than 50 different classical dances are performed in Java and Bali. Most are based on myth, religion, and the great Hindu epics of the *Ramayana* and *Mahabharata*. These dances are usually accompanied by gamelan orchestras and are very popular forms of entertainments for tourists visiting these areas.

DRAMA AND PUPPETRY

Drama in Indonesia usually takes the form of puppetry. *Wayang*, as it is called, is more than a mere spectacle on stage and is probably the most powerful cultural force in the country. In depicting the stories of two great Indian epics, the *Ramayana* and the *Mahabharata*, *wayang* tells of the battle between good and evil, and also explores the strengths and weaknesses of people and society. *Wayang* is an ancient art form that dates back to the eighth century when the epics were incorporated into drama to spread religion. It indirectly teaches about life and all its contradictions, imparts moral values, and provides heroic role models for the young.

A dancer performs the traditional Javanese dance theater piece based on the *Ramayana*.

Characters from the *wayang* are often used to describe personalities: an Arjuna is a good-looking, confident, and loyal person; Rawana embodies deception, evil, and greed; and Semar, one of the oldest and most respected characters, is an honorable name to give someone.

Wayang is so important to Indonesian cultural life that it has in the past been used to transmit government-sponsored messages to villages. *Wayang* performances are exciting, all-night affairs. When a traveling troupe arrives in a village, the entire community gathers to watch.

Behind the scenes of a *wayang kulit* performance: the gamelan sits behind the puppeteer.

"There are those who watch the shadow play, weeping and sad in their foolish understanding, knowing full well that it is really only carved leather which moves and speaks."
—11th-century Javanese poem

Indonesians watch this type of theater in a very different way from how most people watch Western theater. The atmosphere is noisy and informal, where entire families—from grandmothers to young children—relax on mats on the floor and only half-watch the show; everyone is familiar with the ancient stories. *Wayang* watching is a relaxing event where people socialize, catch up on gossip, disappear to have something to eat, doze off when they get tired, and wake up when the gongs begin exciting battle scenes. All this continues into the early hours of the morning when everyone returns home, tired but happy, full of the wonderful stories of "brave heroes and great kingdoms."

The most popular types of drama are *wayang topéng* (masked drama), *wayang kulit* (shadow puppetry), *wayang golék* (wooden puppetry), and *wayang orang* (dance drama). Each of these is a regional specialty and tells of different stories and legends. Although *wayang kulit* and *wayang golék* are usually based on the Hindu epics, in central Java the *wayang golék* tells of popular folk legends based on the spread of Islam.

ARTS AND CRAFTS

Many of Indonesia's arts and crafts are world-famous, especially its *ikat* and batik cloth, sculptures, and beautiful Balinese arts.

TEXTILES Indonesia has a wide range of traditional textiles, from primitive bark cloth, woven *ikat*, and silk *songket*, to sophisticated batik. These are believed to have ritualistic or religious significance. Ikat is used to swaddle the dead, batik is wrapped around a bridal couple to symbolize unity, and the *maa* (mah) cloth of the Torajanese is used only for rituals.

Famous Indonesian textiles include the Sumatran "ship cloths," which depict a scene reminiscent of Noah's Ark with angular-armed people, plants, and animals. These are used to wrap a newborn child, and then for every successive significant event in that person's life, until finally the person dies and the cloth is buried with him or her.

Many of these traditional textiles take a great amount of time and effort to produce. *Ikat*, which requires a traditional method of weaving threads together to create a design, can take up to 10 years to make. Batik production also requires an extraordinary amount of time and patience. This age-old art has been perfected by the Javanese, who produce the finest batik in the world. The intricacy of this art is achieved with the hand-held *canting* (CHAHN-ting), which is used to draw fine wax patterns such as stylized human and animal figures on fabric. The cloth is dyed to color the non-waxed areas, the wax is washed off, and reapplied, and the entire process is repeated until the brilliant detail typical of batik is obtained. A cheaper and faster block printing method is often used today.

Batik designs used to be deeply symbolic, with some reserved for royalty. Today there are more than 1,000 designs with 20 regional styles and countless color combinations.

A woman working a loom in the Batak region.

WOOD SCULPTURE Indonesian wood carving ranges from the primitive tribal statues of Irian Jaya to intricate carvings in Java and Bali. Many of these have won international praise and can be found in art galleries.

JEWELRY Indonesia has a rich tradition of making gold and silver jewelry. The intricate silver jewelry from Bali and Yogyakarta is very popular. The more traditional jewelry includes the gold *mamuli* (mah-moo-lee) pendants from Sumba and the bead necklaces of the Dayaks in Kalimantan.

INDONESIA'S GREATEST WRITER

Pramoedya Ananta Toer (1925—2006) was Indonesia's greatest ever man of letters, with a life and writing career that spanned the entire modern period of Indonesian history. He is famous for writing novels, short stories, essays, and political polemics that address the social, political, and economic concerns of the fledgling Indonesian republic. Born in the town of Blora, in the Java heartland, Pramoedya was involved in nationalist politics from a young age. He wrote propaganda for the nationalist cause during the struggle for independence, and was imprisoned by the Dutch authorities in 1947 for two years. Following independence he worked as a teacher and journalist during the Sukarno era.

Following General Suharto's anti-left-wing coup in 1965, Pramoedya, who headed the People's Cultural Organization (a literary branch of the Indonesian Communist Party), was arrested. He suffered a long period of imprisonment and censorship under the new president Suharto's Order Baru (New Order) in the 1970s and 1980s, and was exiled to the island of Buru for 14 years. Denied writing materials, he composed his most famous work orally while in exile; the Buru Quartet was a series of four historical novels charting the development of Indonesian nationalism from the late 19th century to the 1930s. He was eventually released from Buru in 1979 and lived under house arrest in Jakarta until 1992. During his period of house arrest he became a symbol of human rights abuse and an advocate of free expression in Indonesia.

In his writings he was highly critical of colonialism and the racial and class discrimination of the colonial period. His criticism often extended to the Indonesian government, especially the Suharto regime, which he felt was as exploitative as the Dutch colonial government had been. Most of his writing was banned within Indonesia, although the Buru Quartet and other works were widely read outside Indonesia in translation from the 1980s and have become classics of modern world literature. After Suharto stepped down from power in 1998, Pramoedya was able to travel, making a world tour promoting his memoir, The Mute's Soliloquy. Toward the end of his life he received widespread recognition for his work and many international awards.

BALI'S ART   When people say, "Everyone in Bali is an artist," it is no exaggeration, since it appears that almost every Balinese is involved in creating something artistic. For a small island Bali produces an amazing variety of paintings, sculpture, jewelry, weaving, and other crafts.

The Balinese have been avid painters for the last 400 years, and many have recently won international fame. Their original two- and three-dimensional paintings depict dozens of myths and stories simultaneously on the canvas. The island's sculptors produce everything from slim, elegant, ebony rice-goddesses to fierce, bulging, stone demons that guard all of Bali's crossroads and bridges.

So strong is the artistic atmosphere in Bali that many Western artists have settled there to draw inspiration from its people and culture.

INTERNET LINKS

www.kirjasto.sci.fi/pram.htm

This website offers a brief biography and list of works of Pramoedya Ananta Toer, Indonesia's leading literary figure.

http://homepages.cae.wisc.edu/~jjordan/gamelan/instrum-photo.html

This site includes a photograph showing an entire gamelan orchestra. The site allows you to click on each instrument and see it close up with a description of how it is played.

http://discover-indo.tierranet.com/wayang.html

This site offers an introduction to Indonesian *wayang*, with photographs of elaborate puppets and links describing the mythology and music of *wayang*.

www.indonesiandancefestival.com/

This site covers the biannual dance festival that is held in the Jakarta Institute of the Arts, with photographs and discussion on modern Indonesian dance.

LEISURE

Four boys tussle over a soccer ball. Soccer is one of the most popular games in Indonesia.

11

THE WEEKEND IS AN IMPORTANT time for leisure in Indonesia. People go shopping, visit neighbors and friends, catch up on gossip, and generally relax. Many go for a weekend jaunt to the countryside.

Many Jakartans leave the city and go to seaside resorts such as Anyer on Java's west coast, or take a boat out to the Kepulauan Seribu (Thousand Islands), which is a pretty chain of 105 islands off the coast of Jakarta. Others prefer to leave the heat of the lowlands and go to the hill and mountain resorts. Bogor, Puncak, and Bandung are among the most popular cool weather hill stations with many of Jakarta's residents.

Children in a village play an energetic game of jump rope.

Mischievous children attempting bike stunts.

During celebrations and weekends in Jakarta, traffic is diverted from the main roads to make way for the hoards of residents who stream onto the empty streets for recreation. At daybreak the streets start to fill with children and teenagers playing, dancing, or listening to music; skaters and cyclists; vendors—just about everyone joins in and enjoys the fun. Hawkers set up stalls selling food and the atmosphere becomes that of a street party.

In many villages births, birthdays, weddings, and other life-cycle events are accompanied by elaborate rituals and celebrations.

TRADITIONAL GAMES AND SPORTS

There are numerous traditional games associated with the different islands of Indonesia.

In Nias young men participate in the frightening sport of stone-jumping. The aim is to clear a thick stone wall about 5 feet high by 1.5 feet wide (1.5 m by 0.5 m), sometimes with a sword in hand. After running about

22 yards (20 m) up to the wall, the men jump high into the air, always landing feet first on the other side. These walls, once covered with sharp spikes, were used to train warriors to jump enemy walls while holding a torch in one hand and a sword in the other.

Indonesia is also a nation of seafarers and proud boat-makers: Today boat racing is a colorful tradition on several islands. Balinese men enjoy the sport of cockfighting, while the Madurese spend long hours preparing sleek bulls for their annual bull races.

Some sports are popular all over Indonesia. The sport of *sépak takraw*, which resembles volleyball, is an energetic game where two teams try to keep a plaited rattan ball in the air with their feet. A similar game is *sépak raga*, which is traditional to Sulawesi and Sumatra. Another sport, *pencak silat*, is a form of martial arts that originated in Sumatra, where priests observed and copied the graceful yet lethal movements of animals. When it spread to the royal houses of Java, its deft movements were refined and perfected. Youths of both sexes train themselves in this art today.

Almost every Indonesian enjoys playing *congkak*, a game played with shells or pebbles placed in hollows on a wooden board. This game is especially popular at family gatherings.

The frightening sport of stone-jumping.

MODERN GAMES AND SPORTS

The government's motto "Sports for All" aims to achieve a nation of sports-minded people. A National Sports Day is held every year on September 9, and participants from around the archipelago gather for a week of friendly competition in various sports.

The most popular sports are badminton and soccer. Indonesia is among the premier badminton-playing nations in the world and has won numerous international honors. Rudy Hartono is a living legend in

Indonesia for winning the All England Badminton Championship eight times. Indonesian players have won the Thomas Cup (the world team championship for men's badminton) 13 of the 26 times that it has been held since 1949. At the 1992 Olympic Games in Barcelona, Spain, the Indonesian duo of Susi Susanti and Alan Budikusuma made sports history when they each won a gold medal in the badminton singles final—the first-ever gold medals won by Indonesia at the Olympic Games. Indonesia won one gold and two silver medals in the 2000 Sydney Olympics for badminton, and two silver medals and one bronze medal for weightlifting. At the 2004 Olympic Games in Athens, Taufik Hidayat won the gold medal in men's singles badminton, while at the 2008 Olympics in Beijing Hendra Setiawan and Markis Kido won gold in the men's doubles for badminton.

Boxing and tennis are also extremely popular sports. Indonesia's prize boxer, Ellyas Pical, has won international acclaim, while the nation's tennis team has brought home many regional trophies. Indonesia has also won international medals in table tennis.

Badminton men's doubles champions Markis Kido (*right*) and Hendra Setiawan (*left*) pose for the camera after their win at the 16th Asian Games in 2010.

PASAR MALAM

The night market, or pasar malam, is a way of life in Indonesia. Every town has a night market, selling a delicious range of foods and other goods from temporary stalls. In the larger night markets people can buy anything from clothes, snacks, toys, movie disks, and ornaments, usually at very cheap prices. Often some of the best street food in the area is sold at the night market, with delicious satay, nasi goreng (nah-see GOH-raeng) (fried rice), ayam goreng (fried chicken), as well as numerous types of seafood on sale. For many families the night market is a chance to go out together and eat, shop, see their friends, and see the town, without spending large amounts of money. The pasar malam often happens only one or two days of the week, as the traders rotate around different neighborhoods on different days. Some night markets cater to particular ethnic groups: A Chinese night market might sell mainly Chinese food and Chinese clothing and artifacts, such as mahjong games, while a Javanese night market might sell prayer mats and Malay clothing.

INTERNET LINKS

www.tourdebintan.com/

This site offers a guide to the three-stage Tour de Bintan endurance cycle race on the island of Bintan, covering a total distance of 166 miles (268 km).

www.baliindonesiatours.com/

This tour company site describes many of the most interesting things a tourist can do in the country, including visiting Borobudur and Prambanan, exploring Komodo National Park, experiencing the cultural sites of Bali, and diving.

www.takraw.asia/

This site describes the game of *sépak takraw*, with action photographs of competitive games.

FESTIVALS

Women carrying towers of fruit and
flower offerings at the Mengwi festival.

12

With its diverse religious and ethnic mix, Indonesia celebrates all the major religious festivals as well as many local cultural events.

NDONESIA HAS AN AMAZING array of festivals and celebrations throughout the year, both religious and cultural.

Bali has numerous colorful *odalan* (oh-dahl-anh)—or temple anniversaries—religious holidays, and passage of life ceremonies that involve the whole community. On the island of Java great traditional festivals are held by the royal courts on Islamic holidays. In other parts of Indonesia there are harvest and sea festivals that are a mixture of local traditions and religious beliefs. Cities and towns also celebrate their anniversaries with sports events, traditional art performances, and elaborate processions.

Although Indonesia has official holidays it is not easy to forecast the dates on which these holidays fall, since most of the dates are determined by different calendars. While the European calendar is

Devotees at a Hindu temple gather to usher in the Hindu New Year.

based on the solar year of 365 days, the Muslim calendar is based on the lunar year of 354 days. Thus the dates of Islamic festivals move back about 11 days every solar year. The Balinese and other ethnic groups calculate their calendars in other ways.

Since Indonesia is a Muslim country, most of its public holidays are Muslim festivals. Many of them are also more applicable to Java than to the other islands. But Indonesia also has a Hindu, Buddhist, and Christian population, and there is at least one public holiday for each of these communities.

ISLAMIC FESTIVALS

Lebaran (also called Idul Fitri) is the most important festival in Indonesia, marking the end of the fasting month observed by Muslims.

In the month before Lebaran (called Ramadan), Muslims fast from sunrise to sunset: Adults and children over the age of 10 do not eat or drink anything during daylight hours as a test of their spiritual values and self-discipline. At the end of this fasting month Lebaran is celebrated with noisy festivity throughout the Indonesian archipelago.

Believers carrying a large mound of offering to the main mosque of the city during Garebeg or Sekaten.

People wear new clothes, light firecrackers, prepare elaborate meals at home, and visit friends and relatives bearing gifts of specially prepared cakes and cookies. Streets are filled with people selling colorful cakes and the traditional *ketupat* (kehr-too-paht), woven palm leaves stuffed with steamed rice.

Lebaran celebrations can last from a week to a whole month. At this time people ask forgiveness of their elders and the elder then reciprocates, asking forgiveness of the younger person. The greeting *Selamat Idul Fitri: Ma'afkan Lahir Batin* (Happy Idul Fitri and forgive us for all our wrongdoings) is heard in every home. This festival is also an occasion for paying respects to ancestors. Muslim Indonesians visit family graves to pray and remember their deceased relatives.

Garebeg (also called Sekaten) commemorates the birthday of the Prophet Muhammad and is marked by the biggest religious procession held in Java. Two days before Garebeg large ceremonial food mounds are prepared at the royal palace during the Tumplak Wajik Festival. During Garebeg these mounds are taken in a procession to the main mosque of the city, where they are blessed and distributed to waiting people. It is believed that getting a piece of the *gunungan* (GOO-noong-ahn) or food mound will ensure good fortune and eternal youth, and also guarantee good harvests.

Isra Mi'raj Nabi Muhammad (the Ascension of the Prophet Muhammad) is a time when Muslims celebrate the night when the Archangel Gabriel took the Prophet Muhammad to heaven to speak with God.

Idul Adha is a sacrificial festival when cattle and goats are slaughtered to commemorate Ibrahim's (Abraham) willingness to sacrifice his firstborn son. At this time Muslim pilgrims make the pilgrimage to Mecca. In Indonesia family graves are also visited and cleaned during Idul Adha.

A ceremonial dancer performs on Pemendakan Day, a temple festival.

Hegira, the Islamic New Year, celebrates the day when the Prophet Muhammad made a trip from Mecca to start a new community in Medina, Saudi Arabia, in A.D. 622.

HINDU FESTIVALS

Hindu festivals are celebrated on the Hindu-dominated island of Bali. Nyepi (NEE-ah-pee), the Hindu New Year, is the most important. It is also called the Day of Complete Silence and is spent in prayer and meditation.

The eve of Nyepi, in contrast, is one of the noisiest days on the island. Offerings of wine and meat are laid out at every crossroad to appease the demons believed to reside there. Then, as darkness falls, people come out to the streets beating loud gongs and cymbals, and bearing flaming torches to chase away any remaining demons. Having chased away the evil spirits, everyone spends the next day in total silence, *nyepi*, to make sure that any returning demons will be tricked into believing that Bali is deserted and will

A scary life-sized monster doll, or *ogoh-ogoh*, at Nyepi festivities.

go away. No fires are lit, no work or travel is done, and no one leaves the home.

Galungan is another important Hindu festival in Bali, although it is not one of the official Indonesian holidays. During the 10 days of this festival, it is believed that the gods and revered ancestors return to Earth. The Balinese spend many hours making intricate decorations and place these on the pavement and at the entrances of temples and homes as offerings. Elaborate religious rituals take place in temples simultaneously throughout the island of Bali.

BUDDHIST FESTIVALS

Waisak, the most important festival for Buddhists, celebrates the three most significant moments of the life of the Buddha, founder of the religion—his birth, his moment of enlightenment, and his death.

Thousands gather at the monumental 1,000-year-old Borobudur temple in central Java for this annual celebration. Here a solemn procession of monks carrying flowers and reciting prayers winds its way around the terraces up to the main stupa in what is called the "Noble Silence." Offerings of fresh fruit and flowers are laid out at an ornately decorated altar.

The event climaxes when the moon is at its fullest. Thousands of devotees and monks light candles, meditate, and recite holy verses.

A parade of *barong landung*, or giant puppets, during the Galungan festival.

CHRISTIAN FESTIVALS

Christmas is celebrated in the traditional way among Christians in Indonesia, but Easter is celebrated in an unusual way on the island of Flores.

Wearing dark clothes, triangular white hoods, and costumes reminiscent of 16th-century Portugal, Christians make a barefoot procession through the streets of Flores at midnight. A statue of the Virgin Mary that is said to have washed ashore many years ago and a symbolic black coffin of Jesus are carried along to the beat of muffled drums. With marchers carrying torches and candles and waving grass pom-poms in the air, the procession is an eerie, though fascinating, event to watch.

OTHER FESTIVALS

With the diversity of cultural life in Indonesia's thousands of islands, festivals and celebrations are held all over the country.

The Bull Races of Madura are a colorful and exciting event that takes place after the harvest season. The bulls are fed a diet of chili peppers, honey, beer, and raw eggs. On the day of the race they are brilliantly dressed and paraded through town. Once they reach the stadium, they are raced at speeds of over 30 miles (48 km) per hour down the 110-yard (101-m) track with their jockeys perched behind on wooden sleds. Finally the victorious bull is proudly trotted home to be used as a stud.

A bull rider goads his bulls on during the Bull Races of Madura.

The Kesada Festival is held at the Mount Bromo volcano in east Java. Every year thousands of mountain-dwelling Tenggerese people from the surrounding countryside make a 14-day pilgrimage to Bromo. At a midnight ceremony on the 15th day they offer sacrifices of flowers, rice, chickens, and goats to the goddess of Bromo volcano. According to legend the first ancestor of the Tenggerese sacrificed his 25th child to the volcano goddess in return for abundant crops and many children. Today those who make the pilgrimage to Bromo ask for protection from volcanic eruptions and for good harvests in the coming year.

Kartini Day honors Raden Ajeng Kartini (1879—1904), Indonesia's first campaigner for women's rights and one of its most honored national heroes. On this commemorative day parades, lectures, and school activities are held in her honor. They are attended by women throughout Indonesia, wearing their different regional dresses to symbolize the unity of the nation's women. Also, as on Mother's Day in the West, women are not allowed to work at home—children and fathers take over household chores.

INTERNET LINKS

www.indonesiatravel.org.uk/festivals/

This website lists and describes all the major festivals and holidays in Indonesia, with links showing the calendars for all the major religious festivals as well as descriptions of modern cultural festivals, such as the Kuta Carnival in Bali.

http://balifriend.net/nyepi_day.html

This site offers a detailed description with photographs of Nyepi Day, Bali's annual day of silence.

www.intellasia.net/news/articles/society/111261413.shtml

This is an alternative site that offers coverage of Bali's Nyepi Day, with some colorful photographs of worshipers carrying effigies.

FOOD

A fresh fruit and vegetable stall at a market in Tana Toraja.

13

BECAUSE INDONESIA WAS AT THE crossroads of the ancient trade routes, the nation's cuisine has been shaped by an incredible mixture of foreign influences.

From India came curries and turmeric, from the Chinese came stir-frying and the indispensable wok, and from the Arabs came kebab and other mutton dishes. The Dutch introduced vegetables such as the carrot, tomato, pumpkin, and cauliflower. The Japanese and Thai immigrant cultures have also added variety to Indonesian cuisine.

Surprisingly the traditional spices such as nutmeg, pepper, mace, and cloves for which Indonesia is famous are not commonly used in

The spices on sale at a stall are testament to the foreign influences that have flavored Indonesian cuisine.

Indonesia's spicy cuisine offers a huge variety of dishes that reflect influences from India, China, and Europe, while retaining a flavor and identity all its own.

Indonesian cuisine. Instead the delicate flavor of fresh herbs such as lemon grass, candlenut, and basil are more popular.

Indonesia is home to many tropical fruits, including watermelons, guavas, mangoes, papayas, a variety of bananas, starfruit, avocadoes, *duku* (DOO-koo), rambutan, and durian. The *duku* grows in clusters like bunches of large buff-colored grapes with a thin skin. Inside are five segments of juicy white flesh.

There is also a local remedy for everything from aging to impotence to good skin and weight loss. Called *jamu*, it is commercially produced in Javanese factories from a blend of herbs, minerals, grasses, roots, barks, parts of mammals, birds, reptiles, and jungle plants.

FAVORITE FOODS

Rice is the staple food in most parts of Indonesia and can be eaten for breakfast, lunch, and dinner with either fish, meat, vegetables, or eggs. The popular *nasi goreng* or fried rice is a very popular rice dish. Many snacks and sweet dishes are also made with rice. In the eastern islands of Indonesia, the staple foods are corn, sago, cassava, and sweet potatoes.

Herbal tonics (called *jamu*) for sale. *Jamu* is made from a mix of herbs, spices, and other plant and animal parts.

Fish and other types of seafood are also important food sources in Indonesia. Other favorites are *tahu* (TAH-hoo), or soybean cake, and fermented soybeans wrapped in banana leaf called *tempe* (TAME-pay). These are inexpensive and so rich in protein that they are called the vegetarian meat of the poor. Poultry and eggs are more commonly eaten than red meat.

Coconut is an important ingredient in most Indonesian dishes, adding richness to curries and sauces. Another favorite is a spicy peanut sauce that

RICE—THE SYMBOL OF LIFE

Rice is not just the staple food of Indonesia but is also symbolic of life itself. Images of the rice goddess are found everywhere.

From planting to harvest time the rice crop is carefully nurtured. It is believed that any carelessness will chase away the sacred soul of rice, Dewi Sri, and result in crop failure.

During harvest time care is taken to respect the soul of rice. Harvesters hide their cutting blade in their hand and murmur apologies to Dewi Sri while they cut the rice stalks.

Many of Indonesia's fertility rites involve rice as the symbol of life and continuity. Inverted cones of colored rice are essential for many ceremonies. During major religious festivals decorated mounds of rice are distributed and either eaten or left in the fields to ensure a plentiful harvest.

Sate being grilled.

is poured over salads and accompanies the traditional *sate* (SAH-tay)—pieces of meat seasoned with spices and grilled on bamboo skewers.

Indonesians also make dishes from unusual parts of edible plants such as leaves from bamboo, mango, papaya, cassava, and cashew nut trees, and flowers from the hibiscus plant, banana tree, plus a variety of nuts and seeds.

Most Indonesian food is highly spiced with hot chili peppers or is accompanied by a fiery red chili paste called *sambal* (SAHM-baal). The preparation of *sambal* is such an important part of Indonesian cooking that the cooking skill of young girls is judged according to the quality of *sambal* that they prepare.

Other popular Indonesian dishes are *gado-gado* (gah-doh gah-doh), a vegetable salad served with a peanut sauce, and *bakmi goreng* (buk-mee GOH-rayng) or fried noodles.

DRINKS AND DESSERTS

Indonesian beverages are colorful drinks that are often served as desserts. Among the favorites are creamy fresh avocado juice, sweet perfumed Java tea, and thick black *kopi tubruk* (KOH-pee toh-BROOK), meaning "collision coffee," which is prepared by pouring boiling water onto ground coffee. A refreshing drink is coconut juice drunk straight from a young coconut with its top sliced off. Locally brewed alcoholic drinks are drunk by non-Muslim Indonesians. These include *tuak* (TOO-ahk), or palm wine; *brem* (braem), which is brewed from rice and coconut milk; and *bedek* (bay-DAYK), or rice wine.

TROPICAL FRUIT

There is an amazing array of tropical fruit in Indonesia. Besides the common bananas and pineapples, the country has some unusual produce.

RAMBUTAN This fruit has sweet, translucent, jelly-like flesh, named for its hairy red rind (*rambut* means "hair").

BANANAS They come in all shapes, textures, and sizes, ranging from some that are smaller than an index finger to others over a foot long.

DURIAN This fruit has white, creamy flesh on the inside and a thorny rind outside for which it is named (*duri* means "thorns"). It has a strong smell that takes time to appreciate.

MANGOSTEEN This fruit is purple on the outside with creamy, pure white, fleshy segments inside. Queen Victoria of England promised a reward to anyone who was able to bring some back to England.

SALAK With scaly skin and dry hard flesh, *salak* is similar in taste to an apple.

A colorful selection of fruit, from the bright pink *jambu* (*bottom left*), *belimbing* (starfruit, *top right*), and passion fruit (*bottom, right*).

Indonesians believe that eating with one's hands enhances the flavor of the food.

BLIMBING (STARFRUIT) Starfruit is cool, crisp, and watery inside.

ZURZAT The *zurzat* (whose name is Dutch for "sour-sack") is also called a soursop.

JAMBU AIR This watery, bell-shaped fruit is a thirst quencher.

TABLE MANNERS

Indonesians are very hospitable people and always invite others to join them before starting a meal. To eat without giving a thought to others is considered most uncivilized. Guests are always honored with special treatment. When guests are around the table is laden with far more food than guests can possibly eat.

All the dishes are brought to the table together. Everyone takes a mound of rice on his or her plate and then tries the other dishes with the rice. In rural areas the food is placed on a large woven mat in the center of the kitchen, with everyone sitting cross-legged around it.

The traditional way to eat is with the fingers of the right hand. Indonesians believe that food tastes better when it is eaten by hand rather than with a fork and spoon. They only use their right hand to eat because the left hand is considered unclean. Likewise food should be served and passed with the right hand.

In the cities and towns people do use a fork and spoon. Knives are not necessary since the food is usually cut up into small pieces. Many rural folk still eat with their fingers.

Visitors should learn to wait patiently until they are invited to eat or drink by the host. It is also polite not to finish everything on your plate; if you do it means you are not satisfied and want more.

"In Indonesia it is not sufficient that a man should place good food in front of his guest; he is bound to do more. . . ."
—Sir Stamford Raffles in the 1800s

Traditional herbal remedies, called jamu, *are very popular with Indonesians. These pastes, powders, creams, and capsules are consumed daily and are used to cure everything from headaches and fatigue to leprosy and flabby stomachs.*

These fascinating natural remedies originated in the royal courts of Yogyakarta and Solo. There the ladies of the nobility spent their time discovering and perfecting the science of using roots, flowers, barks, nuts, herbs, and spices to retain their beauty and vigor.

Today these ancient ancestral recipes are used commercially to manufacture a wide variety of jamu *for Indonesians who are firmly convinced of their curative powers.*

KITCHEN UTENSILS

Many kitchen utensils used are particular to Indonesia. Half a coconut shell attached to a split bamboo handle is used as a ladle. The simple wooden mortar and pestle is specially designed to grind the popular *sambal*.

Almost all kitchens have a rice steamer, a special conical steamer made from strips of split bamboo that allows steam from the boiling water below to pass through the rice and cook it.

FOOD PREFERENCES AND TABOOS

Each province or region has different types of food. Javanese food consists of vegetables, soybeans, beef, and chicken, while in the eastern islands, seafood is more important. The Sumatrans eat more beef, while in Bali, Irian Jaya, and northern Sulawesi, pork is more popular. The Muslim population does not eat pork because it is considered unclean, and Muslims also avoid alcohol.

In some regions some unusual dishes may include dog meat, mice, eels, and roasted lizards. Other regional delicacies include *tretis* (TRAY-tis), or partially digested grass from a cow's stomach, dried pork and chicken blood, fried animal skins, and intestines and offal.

Jalan Malioboro in Yogyakarta is famous for having possibly the longest restaurant in the world. Jalan Malioboro is actually one of the main roads in this city, where every evening, vendors line its pavements with bamboo mats and set up food stalls. Customers sit cross-legged on these mats to enjoy traditional gudeg (chicken cooked in jackfruit) and drink clear, sweet tea until the early hours of the morning.

EATING OUT

Eating out is a popular pastime. Indonesians often stop a *kaki lima* (kah-kee LEE-mah) vendor to have a meal on the spot, visit a roadside *warung* (WAH-roong), squat on mats on the street for traditional *gudeg* (gooh-dayg), or choose from a table laden with dishes in a *nasi padang* (literally, "rice of the field") restaurant.

At a *nasi padang* stall like this, diners are allowed to select which dishes they want. The dishes are usually served with rice.

THE _KAKI LIMA_ Named after the 5-foot-wide (1.5-m-wide) sidewalks in Indonesia, _kaki lima_ (literally "five-foot way") are food vendors plying these sidewalks. They carry all their food and cooking utensils in two cabinets hanging from upward-curving bamboo yokes. These colorful vendors have become an institution as Indonesia's mobile restaurants, each using a characteristic cry or sound to attract customers, from the rattle of brass bells to the beating of a Chinese wooden block. When summoned the vendor lowers his wares, squats in front of you, fans his charcoal brazier to a glow, and quickly cooks a dozen sticks of _sate_ or a bowl of noodles on the spot.

WARUNG A _warung_ is the closest Indonesian equivalent to a snack bar. Customers gather to have a drink, order a quick meal cooked on the spot, nibble on snacks, exchange news, or just pass some time. All a _warung_ needs is a roof, a table, a counter to display jars of brightly colored snacks, and a bench for seating.

NASI PADANG Sumatran food from Padang is famous for the variety and number of dishes. In a typical meal the table is laden with a feast of 10 to 25 dishes, and diners can pick and choose what they want.

INTERNET LINKS

www.tasty-indonesian-food.com/index.html
This comprehensive site offers lots of advice on Indonesian food and cooking, including recipes, ingredients, and places to eat.

www.foodbycountry.com/Germany-to-Japan/Indonesia.html
This site describes some popular Indonesian dishes, including fried tofu, fried rice, and fried banana cakes.

www.indochef.com/
This site offers dozens of easy-to-follow Indonesian recipes.

BAMI GORENG (FRIED NOODLES)

0.8 lb (350 g) bami noodles (or other Asian-style noodle)

2 eggs, beaten

3 tablespoons (45 ml) oil

1 lb (450 g) chicken breasts, sliced into ½ inch pieces

2 garlic cloves, minced

2 teaspoons (30 ml) freshly ground coriander

1 teaspoon (15 ml) ground ginger

½ cup (125 ml) vegetable broth

1 onion, sliced into thin wedges

1 carrot, thinly sliced

1 red pepper, thinly sliced

1 leek, thinly sliced

0.4 lb (175 g) ham, cubed

0.3 lb (150 g) shrimp, uncooked

1 tablespoon (15 ml) *sambal oelek* (Indonesian red chili paste)

4—6 tablespoons (60 to 90 ml) *ketjap manis* (Indonesian sweet soya sauce)

Salt & freshly ground black pepper, to taste

Cook noodles according to directions on pack; drain and set aside. Heat a large wok or frying pan and spray with non-stick cooking spray or some cooking oil. Swirl in the beaten egg to make a thin omelet. Remove the egg, cut into thin strips after it is cool, and set aside. Heat oil in a wok. Add the chicken, garlic, coriander, ginger, and broth and saute until the chicken is no longer pink (about 5 to 7 minutes). Add the sliced onion, carrot, red pepper, leek, and *ketjap manis;* sauté 4 to 5 minutes. Add cubed ham, uncooked shrimp, and *sambal oelek;* cook 3 to 4 minutes, or until shrimp turn pink. Add sliced omelet and noodles; mix well and heat thoroughly before serving.

GADO-GADO (MIXED VEGETABLE SALAD WITH PEANUT SAUCE)

Gado-gado is a staple vegetarian dish throughout the country. It is easy to make, healthy, and delicious.

Ingredients:

2 oz. (60 g) bean sprouts (tailed, blanched, drained)

5 oz. (150 g) spinach leaves (boiled, drained)

6 oz. (200 g) bitter gourd (seeded, sliced, boiled)

13 by 3 inch (8 by 8 cm) piece of bean curd (fried, sliced)

13 by 3 inch (8 by 8 cm) piece of fermented soybean (fried, sliced)

3 hard-boiled eggs (sliced)

1—2 tablespoons (15 to 30 ml) of fried shallots

Oyster crackers

You may also use other vegetables in season, such as sliced carrots, string beans, white cabbage, and broccoli.

Peanut sauce:

6 oz. (200 g) peanuts (fried, skin removed, ground)

2 red chilies (ground)

1 teaspoon (5 ml) salt, ground

$1/2$ tablespoon (7.5 ml) brown sugar

0.8 cups (200 ml) water/coconut milk

Mix the peanut sauce ingredients and bring to a boil. Pour peanut sauce over vegetables, fried bean curd, and fermented soybean in a bowl. Garnish with egg slices, a sprinkle of fried shallots, and crushed oyster crackers.

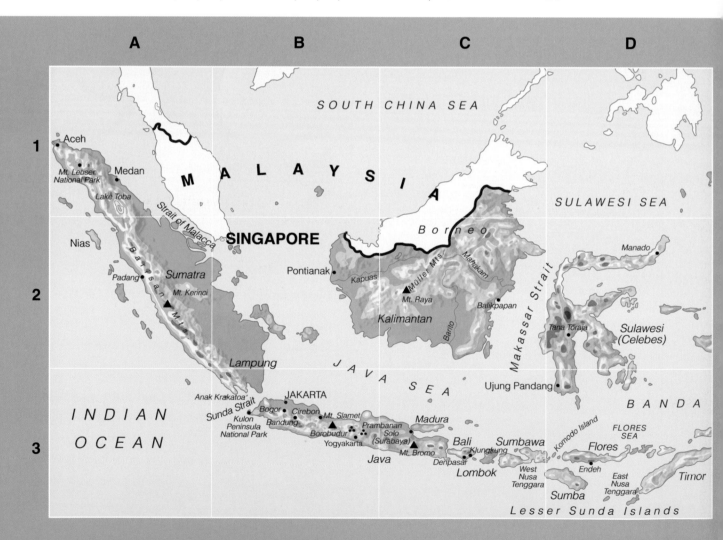

MAP OF INDONESIA

Irian Jaya, E2, F2,
F3

Jakarta, B3
Java, B3, C3
Java Sea, B2, B3, C2,
C3

Jaya Peak, F2

Kalimantan, B2, C1,
C2
Kapuas River, B2,
C2
Klungkung, C3

Komodo Island, D3
Kulon Peninsula
National Park, B3

Lake Toba, A1
Lampung, B2, B3
Lombok, C3

Madura, C3
Mahakam River, C2
Makassar Strait,
C2,
C3, D2
Malaysia, A1, A2,
B1, B2, C1, C2
Moluccas Islands
(Maluku), E2
Manado, D2
Medan, A1
Mount Bromo, C3
Mount Kerinci, A2
Mount Jaya, F2
Mount Leuser
National Park,
A1
Mount Mandula,
F2
Mount Raya, C2
Mount Slamet, B3
Muller Mountains,
C2

Ngga Pilimsit, F2
Nias, A2

Padang, A2
Papua New Guinea,
F2, F3
Pontianak, B2
Prambanan, B3

Singapore, B2
South China Sea,
A1, B1, B2, C1
Strait of Malacca,
A1, A2, B2
Sulawesi (Celebes),
C2, D2, D3
Sulawesi Sea, D1,
D2
Sumatra, A1, A2,
B2, B3
Sumba, D3
Sumbawa, C3
Sunda Strait, B3
Solo (Surabaya), C3

Tana Toraja, D2
Timor, D3, E3

Ujung Pandang, D3

West Nusa
Tenggara, C3

Yogyakarta, B3

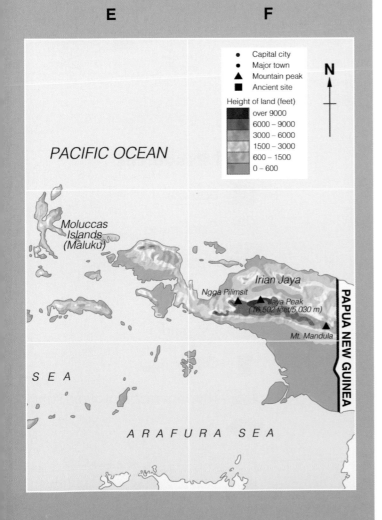

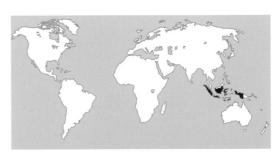

ECONOMIC INDONESIA

Services

 Airport

Ports

Tourism

Agriculture

Coffee/Tea

Corn

Palm oil

Rice

Rubber

Sugarcane

Natural Resources

B Bauxite

Coal mine

Hydroelectic power

Nickel

Oil field

Oil refinery

Thermoelectric powerplant

Timber

Tin

Tin smelter

ABOUT THE ECONOMY

OVERVIEW

The economy of Indonesia is the largest economy in Southeast Asia and one of the biggest emerging economies of the world. It is a member of the G20 organization of major economies. The government plays a significant role in running the economy, and there are numerous large-scale state-run enterprises. The prices of many basic products, such as rice, electricity, and fuel, are controlled by the government. Despite a slow in growth since the global financial crisis and world recession of 2008—10, Indonesia's economy continued to grow at a rate of 6 percent in 2007 and 2008, and over 4 percent in 2009, making it one of the few large economies to expand during the worldwide economic downturn. Indonesia's inadequate infrastructure and corruption continue to hold back the economy, however, as do long-term poverty and unemployment.

GROSS DOMESTIC PRODUCT (GDP)

$962.2 billion (2009 estimate)

GDP PER CAPITA

$4,000 (2009 estimate)

CURRENCY

US$1 = 8,512 Rp (June, 2011)
Indonesian rupiah (Rp) = 100 sen

NATURAL RESOURCES

Petroleum, tin, natural gas, nickel, timber, bauxite, copper, fertile soils, coal, gold, silver

AGRICULTURAL PRODUCTS

Rice, cassava (tapioca), peanuts, rubber, cocoa, coffee, palm oil, copra; poultry, beef, pork, eggs

INFLATION RATE (CONSUMER PRICES)

4.8 percent (2009 estimate)

WORKFORCE

113.7 million (2009 estimate)

UNEMPLOYMENT RATE

8.1 percent (2009 estimate)

EXPORTS

Oil and gas, electrical appliances, plywood, textiles, rubber

EXPORT PARTNERS

Japan: 17.28 percent, Singapore: 11.29 percent, United States: 10.81 percent, China: 7.62 percent, South Korea: 5.53 percent, India: 4.35 percent, Taiwan: 4.11 percent, Malaysia: 4.07 percent (2009 estimate)

MAJOR IMPORTS

Machinery and equipment, chemicals, fuels, foodstuffs

IMPORT PARTNERS

Singapore: 24.96 percent, China: 12.52 percent, Japan: 8.92 percent, Malaysia: 5.88 percent, South Korea: 5.64 percent, United States: 4.88 percent, Thailand: 4.45 percent (2009 estimate)

CULTURAL INDONESIA

Nias
Nias contains a Stone Age civilization which is famous for its woodcarving, dances, and stone-jumping. Stone pedestals, called *hombo batu*, usually about 7 feet (about 2 m) high, were traditionally vaulted by warriors in preparation for battle.

Lake Toba
The largest volcanic lake in the world, Lake Toba is 62 miles (100 km) long, 19 miles (30 km) wide, and 1,666 feet (505 m) at its deepest point. Formed by a gigantic volcanic eruption over 70,000 years ago, the lake today has four visible cones and three craters, as well as a massive island in the center of the lake.

Ujung Kulon Peninsula National Park
Listed as a World Heritage Site by UNESCO, Ujung Kulon is a national park and nature conservation site famous for its pristine tropical rain forest. It is also home to various protected animals, such as the one-horned rhino, banteng, lemur, and a variety of monkeys.

Dieng Plateau
The Dieng Plateau in Java presents an extraordinary landscape; a rich volcanic basin of sulfur springs, lakes, and Hindu temples which are some of Indonesia's oldest remains, dating from the 6th century. Eight (out of a possible 200) small temples remain, originally dedicated to Shiva, the Hindu god of destruction.

Madura
Madura Island is remarkable for the range and style of its traditional sailing vessels, which have a distinctive boomed triangular sail (called a protolateen rig). Such vessels include the *prahu jaring, golekan, lis-alis, leti leti,* and *janggolan*.

Toraja Funerals
The Toraja are famous for their elaborate funerals, which involve vast numbers of guests, sacrifices of buffaloes, dances, parades, and great feasts. Carved life-sized wooden effigies of the dead (*tau tau*) are then set on stone galleries carved out of the cliffs.

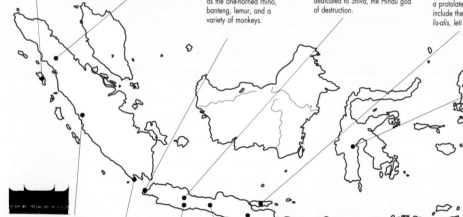

Minangkabau Houses
The matrilineal Minangkabau of West Sumatra are famous for their wooden houses (*rumah gadang*) with curved roofs which look like buffalo horns. Raised 3 to 7 feet (1 to 2 m) off the ground on stilts, the walls are elaborately carved and painted with plant and animal motifs.

Borobudur, Java
This spectacular ninth-century Buddhist monument in central Java consists of nine concentric platforms formed into a broad pyramid. The monument is decorated with 2,672 relief panels and 504 Buddha statues, representing Buddhist cosmology. The upper platform features 72 small stupas (domes) surrounding one large central stupa. Visitors can walk the nine platforms while observing the Buddha's life and Buddhist doctrine as depicted in the panels and sculptures around the platforms.

Mount Krakatau
Located in the Sunda Straits between Sumatra and Java, the famous volcano has a new volcanic peak—Anak Krakatoa (child of Krakatoa)—which surfaced in 1928 and is increasingly active 140 years after the original eruption blew the old peak entirely away.

Prambanan, Java
Prambanan is an impressive ninth-century Hindu temple complex in central Java. Dominated by its imposing 154 feet (47 m) high central building, the temple is dedicated to Trimurti, the expression of God as the Creator (Brahma), the Sustainer (Vishnu) and the Destroyer (Shiva). It is one of the largest Hindu temples in Southeast Asia.

Mount Bromo
Standing at 7,641 feet (2,329 m), this active volcano in East Java is one of the most visited tourist attractions in the region because it constantly belches sulfurous smoke. Local people believe it is home to mountain gods and offerings of food are made during the Hindu festival of Yadnya Kasada.

Ubud
Center of Bali's rich artistic and cultural life, Ubud is located in the foothills of central Bali. Traditionally a refuge for celebrities and artists, today it is at the center of Bali's expanding tourist industry.

Ikat Weaving
Ikat, or resist dyeing, is a technique of cloth patterning found all over Indonesia. Either the warp or the weft is tied with material or fiber to resist the action of the dye. Double *ikat*, however, where both the warp and weft are tie-dyed, is produced in only one place in Southeast Asia—the village of Tenganan in East Bali.

Komodo National Park
The Komodo National Park includes the entire areas of the islands of Komodo, Rinca, and Padar, covering a total surface area of 702 square miles (1,817 square km). Home to the famous Komodo dragon, the park also provides refuge for many other species, such as the orange-footed scrub fowl and the Timor deer. The national park also includes a rich marine environment of coral reefs, over 1,000 species of fish, and other marine life such as sharks, sponges, dugong, and manta rays.

ABOUT THE CULTURE

OFFICIAL NAME
Indonesia

CAPITAL
Jakarta

FLAG
Two equal horizontal bands of red (top) and white

SYSTEM OF GOVERNMENT
Republic

POPULATION
242,968,342 (July 2010 estimate)

ETHNIC GROUPS
Javanese: 40.6 percent, Sundanese: 15 percent, Madurese: 3.3 percent, Minangkabau: 2.7 percent, Betawi: 2.4 percent, Bugis: 2.4 percent, Banten: 2 percent, Banjar: 1.7 percent, other or unspecified: 29.9 percent (2000 census)

RELIGIONS
Muslim: 86.1 percent, Protestant: 5.7 percent, Roman Catholic: 3 percent, Hindu: 1.8 percent, other (animist, unspecified): 3.4 percent (2000 census)

LANGUAGES AND DIALECTS
Bahasa Indonesia (official, modified form of Malay), English, Dutch, local dialects, the most widely spoken of which is Javanese

LITERACY RATE
90.4 percent (2010 estimate)

LIFE EXPECTANCY
Total population: 71.05 years
Male: 68.53 years
Female: 73.69 years (2010 estimate)

NATIONAL ANTHEM
Indonesia Raya (Great Indonesia)

PUBLIC HOLIDAYS AND FESTIVALS
January 1—New Year's Day
February—Chinese New Year
February—Maulid Nabi Muhammad (Birthday of the Prophet Muhammad)
March—Nyepi (Bali)
April—Wafat Isa Al-Masih (Good Friday)
May—Kenaikan Isa Al-Masih (Ascension Day of Jesus Christ)
May—Vesak Day
July—Isra Mi'raj Nabi Muhammad (Ascension Day of the Prophet Muhammad)
August 17—Indonesian Independence Day
November—Idul Adha
December—Islamic New Year
December 25—Christmas Day

TIME LINE

IN INDONESIA	IN THE WORLD
A.D. 600–700 Srivijaya Kingdom is founded.	
778–850 Borobudur is constructed.	
	1206–1368 Genghis Khan unifies the Mongols and starts conquest of the world. At its height, the Mongol Empire under Kublai Khan stretches from China to Persia and parts of Europe and Russia.
1510s Portuguese take control of Maluku.	
1700s Indonesia comes under the control of the Dutch.	**1776** U.S. Declaration of Independence
1811 Java falls to the British East India Company.	**1789–99** The French Revolution
1815–1920 Dutch regain rule over Indonesia.	**1914** World War I begins. **1939** World War II begins.
1945 Proclamation of the independent Republic of Indonesia with Sukarno as its first president.	**1945** The United States drops atomic bombs on Hiroshima and Nagasaki. World War II ends.
1966 Suharto seizes power from Sukarno after a military coup and is appointed president in 1968.	
1998 Suharto steps down.	**1997** Hong Kong is returned to China.
1999 Abdurrahman Wahid declared president and Megawati Sukarnoputri vice president. Referendum in East Timor rejects Indonesian rule.	

IN INDONESIA	IN THE WORLD
2001 Parliament dismisses President Wahid over allegations of corruption. Vice President Megawati Sukarnoputri is sworn in as his replacement.	**2001** Terrorists crash planes into New York, Washington D.C., and Pennsylvania.
2002 East Timor becomes independent. Terrorist bomb in Bali kills 202 people.	
2003 Car bomb in Jakarta kills 14 people.	**2003** War in Iraq begins.
2004 First-ever direct presidential elections: Former general Susilo Bambang Yudhoyono beats standing president Megawati Sukarnoputri. Indian Ocean tsunami kills up to 220,000 people in Indonesia, mainly in Sumatra.	**2004** Eleven Asia countries hit by giant tsunami, killing at least 225,000 people.
2005 Indonesian government signs peace deal with Free Aceh Movement in northern Sumatra.	**2005** Hurricane Katrina devastates the Gulf Coast of the United States.
2006 Earthquake kills thousands in Java.	**2008** Earthquake in Sichuan, China, kills 67,000 people.
2009 President Susilo Bambang Yudhoyono wins re-election.	**2009** Outbreak of flu virus H1N1 around the world
	2011 Twin earthquake and tsunami disasters strike northeast Japan, leaving over 14,000 dead and thousands more missing.

GLOSSARY

adat (AAH-dut)
Customs, traditions, and culture of Indonesian people.

Allahu-akbar (ehl-LAH ho-EHK-behr)
The Muslim muezzin's call to prayer, which means "God is great."

animism
Belief that all natural objects (rocks, trees, and so on) possess spirits.

bahasa (bah-HAH-sah)
Language. Bahasa Indonesia is Indonesia's national language.

batik
Indonesian textile on which patterns are drawn in wax then dyed in colors.

Bhinneka Tunggal Ika (bhee-nay-kah toong-gahl ee-kah)
Unity in Diversity, the national motto.

gamelan
An Indonesian orchestra that plays traditional music.

gotong royong (goh-TOHNG roh-YOHNG)
A concept meaning cooperation or working together as a community.

jamu (JAH-moo)
Traditional herbal tonic.

kasar (KAH-sar)
Unrefined behavior--for example, flailing the arms or speaking in a loud voice.

mandi (MAHN-dee)
A large vat where water is stored for bathing. The word is also used to describe the technique of bathing using the vat of water.

mufakat (moo-FAH-kaht)
Discussion

Salam alaikum (ehs seh-LAHM eh-lei-koom)
A Muslim greeting meaning "Peace be unto you."

sambal (SAHM-baal)
Spicy sauce made from ground chilies and served with rice.

sarong
An ankle-length cloth or skirt worn by both men and women, usually with block patterns.

saudara (sah-hu-DAH-rah)
A term of address meaning "relative of the same generation." Can also be used as an honorable terms of address.

selendang (SER-len-dung)
A long, narrow piece of batik, used as a shawl or a sling.

stupa
Dome enclosing an effigy of the Buddha.

wayang (WAH-young)
Shadow play with leather or flat wooden puppets, usually dramatizing themes from Hindu epics.

FOR FURTHER INFORMATION

BOOKS

Canavan, Roger. *Indonesia (Countries in Crisis)*. Vero Beach, FL: Rourke Publishing, 2008.

Cumming, David. *Indonesia (Letters from Around the World)*. Weybridge, VT: Cherrytree Books, 2009.

Kalman, Bobbie. *Spotlight on Indonesia (Spotlight on My Country)*. New York: Crabtree Publishing Company, 2010.

Lim, Robin. *Indonesia (Country Explorers)*. Minneapolis, MN: Lerner Classroom, 2010.

Phillips, Douglas A. *Indonesia (Modern World Nations)*. New York: Chelsca House Publishers , 2010.

Reusser, Kayleen. *Recipe and Craft Guide to Indonesia (World Crafts and Recipes)*. Hockessin, DE: Mitchell Lane Publishers, 2010.

Ryan, Patrick. *Welcome to Indonesia (Welcome to the World)*. Mankato, MN: Child's World, 2007.

WEBSITES

BBC country profile. http://news.bbc.co.uk/1/hi/world/asia-pacific/country_profiles/1260544.stm

CIA World Factbook. https://www.cia.gov/library/publications/the-world-factbook/geos/id.html

Government of Indonesia. www.indonesia.go.id/en/

Indonesia Tourism. http://indonesia-tourism.com/

Indonesia Traveling over Land, by Sea and the National Parks. www.indonesiatraveling.com/

Jakarta Post. www.thejakartapost.com/

UNESCO. www.unesco.org/new/en/unesco/worldwide/unesco-regions/asia-and-the-pacific/indonesia/

Visit Indonesia. www.indonesia.travel/

BIBLIOGRAPHY

Beatty, Andrew. A *Shadow Falls: In the Heart of Java*. London: Faber & Faber, 2009.

Covarrubias, Miguel. *Island of Bali*. North Clarendon, VT: Periplus Editions, 1999 (originally 1937).

Geertz, Clifford. *The Religion of Java*. Chicago: University of Chicago Press, 1976.

McPhee, Colin. *A House in Bali*. North Clarendon, VT: Periplus Editions, 2000.

O'Rourke, Kevin. *Reformasi: The Struggle for Power in Post-Soeharto Indonesia*. Crows Nest, NSW: Allen & Unwin, 2002.

Robinson, Geoffrey. *The Dark Side of Paradise: Political Violence in Bali*. New York: Cornell University Press, 1995.

Taylor, Jean Gelman. *Indonesia: Peoples and Histories*. New Haven and London: Yale University Press, 2003.

Vickers, Adrian. *A History of Modern Indonesia*. Cambridge: Cambridge University Press, 2005.

Vickers, Adrian. *Bali: A Paradise Created*. North Clarendon, VT: Periplus Editions, 1997.

INDEX

INDEX